金原瑞人
MY FAVORITES

W. SOMERSET MAUGHAM
THE UNCONQUERED SANATORIUM

征服されざる者・サナトリウム

モーム

青灯社

THE UNCONQUERED / SANATORIUM by W. Somerset Maugham

Copyright © The Royal Literary Fund

Japanese translation rights arranged with United Agents Ltd, London
through Tuttle-Mori Agency, Inc., Tokyo

まえがき

1．サマセット・モームの短編ふたつ

　この英語の註釈シリーズもこれで4冊目。今回は、イギリスの20世紀を代表する作家のひとり、サマセット・モームの短編、The Unconquered と Sanatorium を取りあげてみた。「サナトリウム」は現在でも岩波文庫の『モーム短篇選（下）』で読むことができるが、「征服されざる者」は60年以上前に1度訳されたきりで現在入手不可。

　モームやモームの作品の解説はあとがきに回すとして、ここでは英文を読んでいくうえでの注意を書いておこう。

2．文法について

　語注では文法にはほとんど触れていないが、いくつか注意してほしいことがあるので、簡単に書いておきたい。

　「使える英語」とかいう意味不明の言葉が流行し始めて以来、英語の授業から文法や読解の時間が減って、いまや会話中心になってしまった。しかし、小説やエッセイでは口語であまり使われない表現がよく出てくる。

　たとえば分詞構文や仮定法。このふたつは用法が多岐にわたっているので、ここでは説明しないが、不安な方はぜひこれを機会に、文法や読解の参考書を読ん

で勉強してほしい。

　注のなかで、「You（一般人称）」とか「(you は一般人称)」とか出てくる。どういうことかというと、この 'You' は「君、おまえ、あなた」という意味ではなく、人一般を表している。

　たとえば、こんなふうに使う。
・You should be careful when you say 'I love you.'（「愛している」っていうときには、気をつけなくちゃ）
・The older you get, the more you learn about life.（人は年をとればとるほど、人生について多くを学ぶようになる。年をとれば、人生がわかってくるよ）

　本文だと、たとえば、42 ページの 10 行目。

It was true that old Périer had come round. You couldn't say that he was cordial, he was indeed cold and gruff, but he was civil.

　この 'You' は、特定のだれかを指しているわけではない。この場合はただ、'he was cordial' とはいえない、という意味。

　たとえば、64 ページの 18 行目。

You had to admit that, these French people knew how to talk.

　ここも、that 以下のことは認めざるをえないという意味。

　You はよく一般人称として使われるが、'one' が使われることもある。たとえば、120 ページの 12 行目。

once she had come he seemed less pleased than one would have expected.

こういう 'you' や 'one' に慣れておくと、小説を読むのが少し楽になる。

それからもうひとつ、It is (was)...that の強調構文も会話ではあまり使われないので、苦手な人が多い。モームの短編にもよく出てくるので、簡単に説明しておこう。

たとえば "He met Hans yesterday." という文のうち、'he' 'Hans' 'yesterday' の3つをそれぞれ強調したい場合、次のように表現する。

・It was he that met Hans yesterday.（昨日ハンスに会ったのは彼だ）
・It was Hans that he met yesterday.（彼が昨日会ったのはハンスだ）
・It was yesterday that he met Hans.（彼がハンスに会ったのは昨日だ）

It is (was)...that の強調構文を、It が that 以下を受けていると勘違いすると意味がわからなくなるので注意してほしい。この強調構文、上の例のように単純な場合は気がつきやすいが、文が長くなったり複雑になったりすると、案外と難しい。この註釈本でも何カ所か、指摘しておいた。

たとえば、「サナトリウム」の122ページの22行目。

It's when I'm here, when he sees me well and strong, that it comes over him.

これも強調構文。

それから会話でほとんど使われないけれど、小説などでは描出話法もよく使われる。たとえば、22ペー

ジの9行目からの段落。

He put his hands over the girl's mouth to stop her shrieking and carried her out of the room. That was how it had happened and you had to admit that she'd brought it on herself. She shouldn't have slapped him.

この段落の最初の1行は、普通の描写の文だが、その次からは、ハンスの考えていること。

(彼は両手で娘の口をふさいで悲鳴を抑え、その部屋から連れ出した。こんなことになったのも、自業自得ってやつだ。おれを引っぱたいたりしなきゃよかったんだ)

ちなみに、'you had to admit' の 'you' も一般人称。

3. 舞台、その他について

「征服されざる者」。時代は第2次世界大戦で、ドイツがフランスに侵攻してしばらくした頃。舞台は、フランス北部の都市ソアソン。その町に侵攻してきたドイツ軍の兵士、ハンスが主人公。仲間とふたりで、フランス人の農家に押しかけて、ワインを飲んでいるうちに、そこの家の娘が生意気なのにいらだって、暴行におよぶ……ところが、それがきっかけになって、物語は思いもよらない方向に進みだす。

「サナトリウム」。時代は第1次世界大戦後。スコットランド北部にあるサナトリウムで暮らす人々の人間模様を、そこにやってきたアシェンデンの目を通して描いている。アシェンデンは『アシェンデン』という連作短編集の主人公でイギリスの諜報部員。モーム自

身、第1次世界大戦中、諜報活動をしたことがあり、また結核でサナトリウムに入院していたこともある。そのときの体験をもとに書かれたらしい。

　生きることの残酷さを目の当たりにみせるような短編と、ドラマティックな展開のなかに人間味豊かな味わいを感じさせる短編の2本立て。味わいはまったくちがうが、どちらも、じつにモームらしい、よく練られた短編だ。短編の楽しさを十分に味わってほしい。

金原瑞人

contents

まえがき　金原瑞人 ………· 3

The Unconquered ………· 11

Sanatorium ………· 95

あとがき　金原瑞人 ………· 169

装幀　眞島和馬

The Unconquered

He came back into the kitchen. The man was still on the floor, lying where he had hit him, and his face was bloody. He was moaning. The woman had backed against the wall and was staring with terrified eyes at Willi, his friend, and when he came in she gave a gasp and broke into loud sobbing. Willi was sitting at the table, his revolver in his hand, with a half empty glass of wine beside him. Hans went up to the table, filled his glass and emptied it at a gulp.

'You look as though you'd had trouble, young fellow,' said Willi with a grin.

Hans's face was blood-stained and you could see the gashes of five sharp finger-nails. He put his hand gingerly to his cheek.

'She'd have scratched my eyes out if she could, the bitch. I shall have to put some iodine on. But she's all right now. You go along.'

'I don't know. Shall I? It's getting late.'

'Don't be a fool. You're a man, aren't you? What if it is getting late? We lost our way.'

It was still light and the westering sun streamed into the kitchen windows of the farm-house. Willi hesitated a moment. He was a little fellow, dark and thin-faced, a dress designer in civil life, and he didn't want Hans to think him a cissy. He got up and went towards the door through which Hans had come. When the woman saw what he was going to do she gave a shriek and sprang forwards.

'*Non, non,*' she cried.

The Unconquered

1 He ドイツ軍の兵士ハンス The man フランス人の娘、アネットの父親 2 he ハンス him 父親 his 父親の 3 moaning うめいている The woman アネットの母親 backed 後ずさった 4 against the wall 壁にもたれて 5 his ハンスの gasp あえぎ 6 sobbing すすり泣き 8 Hans ハンス 9 at a gulp 一気に

10 you'd had trouble おまえ、手こずったようだな 11 grin 歯を見せて笑うこと

12 blood-stained 血に濡れている 13 gashes 深い傷 gingerly そっと

15 She'd have scratched my eyes out (She'd は She could で、仮定法) もし可能だったら、あの娘はおれの目玉をえぐりだしただろう the bitch あばずれ 16 some iodine ヨードチンキ she's all right now いまはもうだいじょうぶだ 17 You go along おまえもいってこい

18 Shall I? おれにいけって？

19 What if it is getting late? おそくなったから、どうだっていうんだ？ 20 We lost our way おれたちは道に迷ったんだから

21 westering 西に傾く streamed into 射しこんでいた

22 farm-house 農家 23 dark and thin-faced 色黒で細面

24 dress designer in civil life 平時（兵士になる前）はデザイナー

25 cissy 女みたいな 27 shriek 叫び声 sprang forwards 前に飛びだした

13

With one step Hans was in front of her. He seized her by the shoulders and flung her violently back. She tottered and fell. He took Willi's revolver.

'Stop still, both of you,' he rasped in French, but with his guttural German accent. He nodded his head towards the door. 'Go on. I'll look after them.'

Willi went out, but in a moment was back again.

'She's unconscious.'

'Well, what of it?'

'I can't. It's no good.'

'Stupid, that's what you are. *Ein Weibchen*. A woman.'

Willi flushed.

'We'd better be getting on our way.'

Hans shrugged a scornful shoulder.

'I'll just finish the bottle of wine and then we'll go.'

He was feeling at ease and it would have been pleasant to linger. He had been on the job since morning and after so many hours on his motor-cycle his limbs ached. Luckily they hadn't far to go, only to Soissons — ten or fifteen kilometres. He wondered if he'd have the luck to get a bed to sleep in. Of course all this wouldn't have happened if the girl hadn't been a fool. They had lost their way, he and Willi, they had stopped a peasant working in a field and he had deliberately misled them, and they found themselves on a side road. When they came to the farm they stopped to ask for a direction. They'd asked very politely, for orders were to treat the French population well as long as they behaved them-

2 **flung...back** 後ろに投げ飛ばした　**tottered** よろけた
4 **Stop still** 動くな　**rasped** 耳障りな声で怒鳴った　5 **guttural** 喉の奥から出るような　**German accent** ドイツ語訛り　**nodded his head towards the door** ドアのほうにむかってうなずいた　6 **Go on** 行けよ
8 **unconscious** 気を失っている
9 **what of it?** それがどうした？
10 **I can't** 自分にはできない　**It's no good** まずいだろう
11 **Ein Weibchen** 'A woman' のドイツ語
13 **flushed** 赤くなった
14 **getting on our way** (部隊が駐屯しているところに) もどる
15 **shrugged a scornful shoulder** ばかにしたように肩をすくめた
17 **He** ハンス　**feeling at ease** ほっとする　18 **linger** 休んでいく　19 **his limbs** 全身　20 **Soissons** ソアソン (フランス北部の古都)　21 **have the luck to** 運よく to 以下のようになる　22 **all this wouldn't have happened** (仮定法) こんなことは起こらなかっただろう　24 **a peasant** 農夫　25 **in a field** 畑で　**deliberately** わざと　**misled** 違う方向を教えた　26 **a side road** 脇道　28 **for** なぜなら　**orders** (軍からの) 命令　**treat the French population well** フランス人には親切にする　29 **as long as they behaved themselves** 彼らがおとなしくしている限りは

selves. The door was opened for them by the girl and she said she didn't know the way to Soissons, so they pushed in; then the woman, her mother, Hans guessed, told them. The three of them, the farmer, his wife and daughter, had just finished supper and there was a bottle of wine on the table. It reminded Hans that he was as thirsty as the devil. The day had been sweltering and he hadn't had a drink since noon. He asked them for a bottle of wine and Willi had added that they would pay them well for it. Willi was a good little chap, but soft. After all, they were the victors. Where was the French army? In headlong flight. And the English, leaving everything behind, had scuttled like rabbits back to their island. The conquerors took what they wanted, didn't they? But Willi had worked at a Paris dressmaker's for two years. It's true he spoke French well, that's why he had his present job, but it had done something to him. A decadent people. It did a German no good to live among them.

The farmer's wife put a couple of bottles of wine on the table and Willi took twenty francs out of his pocket and gave it to her. She didn't even say thank you. Hans's French wasn't as good as Willi's, but he could make himself understood, and he and Willi spoke it together all the time. Willi corrected his mistakes. It was because Willi was so useful to him in this way that he had made him his friend, and he knew that Willi admired him. He admired him because he was so tall, slim, and broad-shouldered, because his curly hair was so fair and his

3 **pushed in** 家の中に押し入った   **her mother, Hans guessed** 彼女の母親だろうとハンスは思った   7 **as...as the devil**（強調）とても   **sweltering** 汗だくになる   9 **pay them well** 彼らに十分金を払う   10 **good little chap** いいやつ   **soft** 意気地がない   11 **victors** 勝利者   **Where was the French army?** フランス軍はどこにいる？   12 **headlong flight** 必死の逃亡   **the English, leaving everything behind, had scuttled** イギリス軍は、すべてを置いて、逃げていった   13 **back to their island** 自分たちの島へ   14 **conquerors** 征服者たち（ドイツ軍）   16 **that's why** そのおかげで   17 **it had done something to him** それ（パリで働いていたこと）は彼に影響をおよぼした   18 **decadent** 退廃的な、遊び好きで怠惰な   **It did a German no good to live among them** It は to 以下（フランス人の間で暮らすこと）
21 **francs** フラン（当時のフランスの通貨）   23 **make himself understood** 自分のいいたいことを伝える   24 **it** フランス語   28 **broad-shouldered** 肩幅が広い   29 **fair** 美しい金髪

eyes so blue. He never lost an opportunity to practise his French, and he tried to talk now, but those three French people wouldn't meet him half-way. He told them that he was a farmer's son himself and when the war was over was going back to the farm. He had been sent to school in Munich because his mother wanted him to go into business, but his heart wasn't in it, and so after matriculating he had gone to an agricultural college.

'You came here to ask your way and now you know it,' said the girl. 'Drink up your wine and go.'

He had hardly looked at her before. She wasn't pretty, but she had fine dark eyes and a straight nose. Her face was very pale. She was plainly dressed, but somehow she didn't look quite like what she evidently was. There was a sort of distinction about her. Ever since the war started he'd heard fellows talk about the French girls. They had something the German girls hadn't. Chic, Willi said it was, but when he asked him just what he meant by that Willi could only say that you had to see it to understand. Of course he'd heard others say that they were mercenary and hard as nails. Well, they'd be in Paris in a week and he'd find out for himself. They said the High Command had already arranged for houses for the men to go to.

'Finish your wine and let's go,' said Willi.

But Hans was feeling comfortable and didn't want to be hurried.

'You don't look like a farmer's daughter,' he said to the girl.

The Unconquered

3 **meet him half-way** 妥協する 6 **Munich** ミュンヘン（ドイツの都市） **go into business** 商売をする 7 **matriculating** 大学の入学資格取得 8 **an agricultural college** 農業大学 12 **a straight nose** 鼻筋が通っている 13 **pale** 色白 **plainly dressed** 質素な服を着ている 14 **what she evidently was** 実際に目に映る彼女 15 **distinction** 非凡さ、気品、個性 17 **Chic** 上品さ、垢抜けた感じ 18 **what he meant by that** (that は Chic) シックって、どういうことなのか 19 **you had to see it to understand** それを理解するには自分の目で確かめるしかない 21 **mercenary** 傭兵、この場合は「金銭にいやしい人間」 **hard as nails** 薄情な 22 **he'd find out for himself** 自分でわかるだろう 23 **High Command** 最高司令部 **houses** 売春宿、慰安所

'And so what?' she answered.

'She's a teacher,' said her mother.

'Then you've had a good education.' She shrugged her shoulders, but he went on good-humouredly in his bad French. 'You ought to understand that this is the best thing that has ever happened to the French people. We didn't declare war. You declared war. And now we're going to make France a decent country. We're going to put order into it. We're going to teach you to work. You'll learn obedience and discipline.'

She clenched her fists and looked at him, her eyes black with hatred. But she did not speak.

'You're drunk, Hans,' said Willi.

'I'm as sober as a judge. I'm only telling them the truth and they may just as well know it at once.'

'He's right,' she cried out, unable any longer to contain herself. 'You're drunk. Now go. Go.'

'Oh, you understand German, do you? All right, I'll go. But you must give me a kiss first.'

She took a step back to avoid him, but he seized her wrist.

'Father,' she cried. 'Father.'

The farmer flung himself on the German. Hans let go of her and with all his might hit him in the face. He crumpled up on the floor. Then, before she could escape him, he caught the girl in his arms. She gave him a swinging blow on the cheek . . . He chuckled grimly.

'Is that how you take it when a German soldier wants to kiss you? You'll pay for this.'

The Unconquered

1 **so what?** だからなによ？ 3 **a good education** しっかりした教育 4 **good-humouredly** 陽気に 8 **decent** 礼儀正しい 9 **put order into it** フランスに秩序をもたらす 10 **obedience** 従順さ **discipline** 規律
11 **clenched her fists** 両手を握りしめる
14 **sober as a judge** 判事くらい（とても）素面だ 15 **may just as well know it** 理解できたほうがいい
16 **contain herself** 自分をおさえる
20 **seized** つかんだ
23 **flung himself** 飛びかかった **let go of her** 彼女を放した
24 **with all his might** 思いきり 25 **crumpled up** 力なく倒れた
27 **swinging blow** 力を込めた一発 **chuckled grimly** 不気味な笑い声をあげた
28 **Is that how you take it** それがおまえの返事か 29 **pay for this** 思い知らせてやる

With his great strength he pinioned her arms and was dragging her out of the door, but her mother rushed at him and catching him by the clothes tried to pull him away. With one arm holding the girl close to him, with the flat of his other hand he gave the woman a great push and she staggered back to the wall.

'Hans, Hans,' cried Willi.

'Shut up, damn you.'

He put his hands over the girl's mouth to stop her shrieking and carried her out of the room. That was how it had happened and you had to admit that she'd brought it on herself. She shouldn't have slapped him. If she'd given him the kiss he'd asked for he'd have gone away. He gave a glance at the farmer still lying where he had fallen and he could hardly help laughing at his funny face. There was a smile in his eyes when he looked at the woman cowering against the wall. Was she afraid it was her turn next? Not likely. He remembered a French proverb.

'*C'est le premier pas qui coûte*. There's nothing to cry about, old woman. It had to come sooner or later.' He put his hand to his hip pocket and pulled out a wallet. 'Look, here's a hundred francs so that mademoiselle can buy herself a new dress. There's not much left of that one.' He placed the note on the table and put his helmet back on his head. 'Let's go.'

They slammed the door behind them and got on their motorcycles. The woman went into the parlour. Her daughter was lying on the divan. She was lying as he

1 **pininoned her arms** 彼女を羽交い締めにした 3 **catching him by the clothes** 彼の服をつかんで 5 **flat of his other hand** もう一方の掌で 6 **staggered** よろめいた
8 **damn you** (相手をののしるときの言葉) ばか野郎
10 **shrieking** 叫ぶこと 11 **you had to admit that** (you は一般人称) that 以下のことは認めなくちゃいけない。(ここはハンスの考えがそのまま地の文で表現されている) **she'd brought it on herself** 自業自得だ 13 **the kiss he'd asked for** 彼が望んだキス 15 **could hardly help laughing** 思わず笑ってしまった
17 **cowering** すくんでいる 18 **her turn next** 次は自分の番
20 **C'est le premier pas qui coûte** つらいのは最初だけだ
23 **that mademoiselle** あの女の子 24 **There's not much left of that one** (that one は女の子の着ている dress) あの服はもうぼろぼろだ 25 **the note** 100 フラン紙幣
28 **parlour** 客間 29 **divan** ソファ

had left her and she was weeping bitterly.

Three months later Hans found himself in Soissons again. He had been in Paris with the conquering army and had ridden through the Arc de Triomphe on his motorcycle. He had advanced with the army first to Tours and then to Bordeaux. He'd seen very little fighting. The only French soldiers he'd seen were prisoners. The campaign had been the greatest spree he could ever have imagined. After the armistice he had spent a month in Paris. He'd sent picture postcards to his family in Bavaria and bought them all presents. Willi, because he knew the city like the palm of his hand, had stayed on, but he and the rest of his unit were sent to Soissons to join the force that was holding it. It was a nice little town and he was comfortably billeted. Plenty to eat and champagne for less than a mark a bottle in German money. When he was ordered to proceed there it had occurred to him that it would be fun to go and have a look at the girl he'd had. He'd take her a pair of silk stockings to show there was no ill-feeling. He had a good bump of locality and he thought he would be able to find the farm without difficulty. So one afternoon, when he had nothing to do, he put the silk stockings in his pocket and got on his machine. It was a lovely autumn day, with hardly a cloud in the sky, and it was pretty, undulating country that he rode through. It had been fine and dry for so long that, though it was September, not even the restless poplars gave sign that the summer was drawing to an end. He took one wrong turning, which delayed him, but for

The Unconquered

1 **bitterly** 激しく
2 **found himself in Soissons again** またソアソンにきていた
4 **Arc de Triomphe** 凱旋門 **motorcycle** オートバイ 5 **Tours** トゥール（フランス中北西部の古都） 6 **Bordeaux** ボルドー（フランス南西部の河港都市。ワインの産地） **The only French soldiers he'd seen** 彼が目にした唯一のフランス兵 7 **The campaign** あの軍事行動（フランスへの侵攻） 8 **spree** 大騒動 9 **armistice** 休戦 10 **Bavaria** バイエルン（ドイツ南東部の州） 13 **unit** 部隊 14 **force** 軍隊 **was holding it** ソアソンを占領している 15 **billeted** 宿舎を割り当てられる 16 **less than a mark a bottle** 1本1マルク（マルクは当時のドイツの通貨）しない 17 **proceed** おもむく 19 **he'd had** 彼が犯した **to show there was no ill-feeling** 悪気はなかったことを示す 20 **a good bump of locality** 土地勘がある 24 **machine** バイク **with hardly a cloud in the sky** 空にはほとんど雲がない 25 **undulating** ゆるやかな起伏がある 27 **restless** 季節の移り変わりに敏感な **poplars** ポプラ 28 **drawing to an end** 終わりに近づいている

all that he got to the place he sought in less than half an hour. A mongrel dog barked at him as he walked up to the door. He did not knock, but turned the handle and stepped in. The girl was sitting at the table peeling potatoes. She sprang to her feet when she saw the uniformed man.

'What d'you want?' Then she recognized him. She backed to the wall, clutching the knife in her hands. 'It's you. *Cochon.*'

'Don't get excited. I'm not going to hurt you. Look. I've brought you some silk stockings.'

'Take them away and take yourself off with them.'

'Don't be silly. Drop that knife. You'll only get hurt if you try to be nasty. You needn't be afraid of me.'

'I'm not afraid of you,' she said.

She let the knife fall to the floor. He took off his helmet and sat down. He reached out with his foot and drew the knife towards him.

'Shall I peel some of your potatoes for you?' She did not answer. He bent down for the knife and then took a potato out of the bowl and went to work on it. Her face hard, her eyes hostile, she stood against the wall and watched him. He smiled at her disarmingly. 'Why do you look so cross? I didn't do you much harm, you know. I was excited, we all were, they'd talked of the invincible French army and the Maginot line . . .' he finished the sentence with a chuckle. 'And the wine went to my head. You might have fared worse. Women have told me that I'm not a bad-looking fellow.'

2 **A mongrel dog** 雑種犬　5 **sprang to her feet** ぱっと立ち上がった　**the uniformed man** 軍服姿の男
7 **recognized him** 彼を覚えていた　8 **clutching** 握りしめて
9 **Cochon** 豚
12 **Take them away** そんなもの持って帰って
13 **You'll only get hurt** 痛い目をみるだけだ　14 **nasty** いやな態度を取る
17 **reached out with his foot** 足を伸ばした
22 **hostile** 敵意に満ちている　23 **disarmingly** 相手を安心させるように　24 **cross** 物騒な、不機嫌な　26 **invincible** 無敵の　**Maginot line** マジノ線（ドイツ軍の侵攻を防ぐためにフランスが築いた大要塞線。スイスからベルギーにかけての国境地帯、400kmにわたっていた。しかし1940年、ドイツ軍の電撃作戦で突破された）　27 **chuckle** にやにや笑い　**the wine went to my head** ワインで理性がなくなっていた　28 **might have fared worse** もっとひどいことになっていたかもしれない　29 **bad-looking** 見栄えの悪い

She looked him up and down scornfully.

'Get out of here.'

'Not until I choose.'

'If you don't go my father will go to Soissons and complain to the general.'

'Much he'll care. Our orders are to make friends with the population. What's your name?'

'That's not your business.'

There was a flush in her cheeks now and her angry eyes were blazing. She was prettier than he remembered her. He hadn't done so badly. She had a refinement that suggested the city-dweller rather than the peasant. He remembered her mother saying she was a teacher. Because she was almost a lady it amused him to torment her. He felt strong and healthy. He passed his hand through his curly blond hair, and giggled when he thought that many girls would have jumped at the chance she had had. His face was so deeply tanned by the summer that his eyes were startlingly blue.

'Where are your father and mother?'

'Working in the fields.'

'I'm hungry. Give me a bit of bread and cheese and a glass of wine. I'll pay.'

She gave a harsh laugh.

'We haven't seen cheese for three months. We haven't enough bread to stay our hunger. The French took our horses a year ago and now the Boches have taken our cows, our pigs, our chickens, everything.'

'Well, they paid you for them.'

The Unconquered

3 **Not until I choose** おれがそう決めるまでは、出ていかない
5 **general** 軍司令官
6 **Much he'll care** 彼は大いに気をつかってくれるだろう（皮肉）
7 **the population** フランス人
9 **flush** 赤味　10 **blazing** 燃えている　12 **city-dweller** 都会の人間　14 **almost a lady** 貴婦人に近い　**torment** いじめる　16 **giggled** 笑い声をもらした　17 **would have jumped at the chance** （仮定法）こういうチャンスに飛びついただろう　18 **tanned** 日焼けしている　19 **startlingly** 驚くほど
24 **harsh** 耳障りな、かん高い
26 **stay** おとなしくさせる　**The French** フランス兵　27 **the Boches** ドイツ兵

'Can we eat the worthless paper they gave us?'

She began to cry.

'Are you hungry?'

'Oh, no,' she answered bitterly, 'we can eat like kings on potatoes and bread and turnips and lettuce. Tomorrow my father's going to Soissons to see if he can buy some horse meat.'

'Listen, Miss. I'm not a bad fellow. I'll bring you a cheese, and I think I can get hold of a bit of ham.'

'I don't want your presents. I'll starve before I touch the food you swine have stolen from us.'

'We'll see,' he said good-humouredly.

He put on his hat, got up, and with an *Au revoir, mademoiselle*, walked out.

He wasn't supposed to go joy-riding round the country and he had to wait to be sent on an errand before he was able to get to the farm again. It was ten days later. He walked in as unceremoniously as before and this time he found the farmer and his wife in the kitchen. It was round about noon and the woman was stirring a pot on the stove. The man was seated at table. They gave him a glance when he came in, but there was no surprise in it. Their daughter had evidently told them of his visit. They did not speak. The woman went on with her cooking, and the man, a surly look on his face, stared at the oil-cloth on the table. But it required more than this to disconcert the goodhumoured Hans.

'*Bonjour, la compagnie*,' he said cheerfully. 'I've brought you a present.'

5 **turnips** カブ
9 **get hold of** 手に入れる
11 **you swine** あんたのような豚
12 **We'll see** どうなるか、拝見しよう　**good-humouredly** 陽気に
13 **Au revoir, mademoiselle** =Goodbye, lady
15 **wasn't supposed to** to 以下のことができなかった　**joy-riding** のんびりバイクを乗り回す　16 **be sent on an errand** 使いに出される　18 **unceremoniously** 無遠慮に　20 **round about noon** 正午近く　**stirring** かき回す　25 **surly look** むっつりした表情　26 **oil-cloth** 油布　**it required more than this to disconcert the goodhumoured Hans** (it は to 以下) 陽気なハンスをたじろがせるには、これ (冷ややかな目を向けられていること) 以上のことが必要だった→陽気なハンスは、これくらいのことではたじろがなかった
28 **Bonjour, la compagnie** こんにちは、みなさん

He undid the package he had with him and set out a sizable piece of Gruyère cheese, a piece of pork, and a couple of tins of sardines. The woman turned round and he smiled when he saw the light of greed in her eyes. The man looked at the foodstuff sullenly. Hans gave him his sunny grin.

'I'm sorry we had a misunderstanding the first time I came here. But you shouldn't have interfered.'

At that moment the girl came in.

'What are you doing here?' she cried harshly. Then her eyes fell on the things he had brought. She swept them together and flung them at him. 'Take them away. Take them.'

But her mother sprang forward.

'Annette, you're crazy.'

'I won't take his presents.'

'It's our own food that they've stolen from us. Look at the sardines. They're Bordeaux sardines.'

She picked the things up. Hans looked at the girl with a mocking smile in his light blue eyes.

'Annette's your name, is it? A pretty name. Do you grudge your parents a little food? You said you hadn't had cheese for three months. I couldn't get any ham; I did the best I could.'

The farmer's wife took the lump of meat in her hands and pressed it to her bosom. You felt that she could have kissed it. Tears ran down Annette's cheeks.

'The shame of it,' she groaned.

'Oh, come now, there's no shame in a bit of Gruyère

1 **undid** 開ける 2 **sizable** 大きな **Gruyère cheese** グリュイエルチーズ（牛乳から作ったチーズ。スイスのグリュイエール地方特産） 3 **tins of sardines** イワシの稚魚の缶詰 4 **greed** 物欲しそうな表情 5 **foodstuff** チーズのこと **sullenly** むっつりと 6 **sunny grin** 明るい微笑み
8 **interfered** 干渉する、邪魔をする
11 **swept them together** かき集めた
15 **Annette** アネット（娘の名前）
20 **mocking** からかうような
22 **grudge** 与えることをいやがる
25 **lump** 塊 26 **You**（一般人称）
28 **The shame of it** みっともない、恥ずかしい **groaned** いやそうな声でいう
29 **come now** まあまあ、これこれ

and a piece of pork.'

Hans sat down and lit a cigarette. Then he passed the packet over to the old man. The farmer hesitated for a moment, but the temptation was too strong for him; he took one and handed back the packet.

'Keep it,' said Hans. 'I can get plenty more.' He inhaled the smoke and blew a cloud of it from his nostrils. 'Why can't we be friends? What's done can't be undone. War is war, and, well, you know what I mean. I know Annette's an educated girl and I want her to think well of me. I expect we shall be in Soissons for quite a while and I can bring you something now and then to help out. You know, we do all we can to make friends with the townspeople, but they won't let us. They won't even look at us when we pass them in the street. After all, it was an accident, what happened that time I came here with Willi. You needn't be afraid of me. I'll respect Annette as if she was my own sister.'

'Why do you want to come here? Why can't you leave us alone?' asked Annette.

He really didn't know. He didn't like to say that he wanted a little human friendship. The silent hostility that surrounded them all at Soissons got on his nerves so that sometimes he wanted to go up to a Frenchman who looked at him as if he wasn't there and knock him down, and sometimes it affected him so that he was almost inclined to cry. It would be nice if he had some place to go where he was welcome. He spoke the truth when he said he had no desire for Annette. She wasn't

2 **the packet** タバコの箱 4 **temptation** 誘惑
7 **inhaled** 吸う **nostrils** 鼻孔 8 **What's done can't be undone** してしまったことはもとにもどすことはできない
10 **think well of me** 自分のことをよく思う 14 **won't let us**（あとに make friends with が省略されている）そうさせてくれない
15 **pass** 通りかかる
20 **leave us alone** わたしたちにかまわないでいる
22 **hostility** 敵意 23 **got on his nerves** 神経に障ってきた
25 **looked at him as if he wasn't there** まるで彼がそこにいないかのような目で彼をみた **knock him down** 殴り倒す 27 **inclined to cry** 泣きたい気持ちになった 29 **desire** 欲望

the sort of woman he fancied. He liked women to be tall and full-breasted, blueeyed, and fair-haired like himself; he liked them to be strong and hefty and well-covered. That refinement which he couldn't account for, that thin fine nose and those dark eyes, the long pale face — there was something intimidating about the girl, so that if he hadn't been excited by the great victories of the German armies, if he hadn't been so tired and yet so elated, if he hadn't drunk all that wine on an empty stomach, it would never have crossed his mind that he could have anything to do with her.

For a fortnight after that Hans couldn't get away. He'd left the food at the farm and he had no doubt that the old people had wolfed it. He wondered if Annette had eaten it too; he wouldn't have been surprised to discover that the moment his back was turned she had set to with the others. These French people, they couldn't resist getting something for nothing. They were weak and decadent. She hated him, yes, God, how she hated him, but pork was pork, and cheese was cheese. He thought of her quite a lot. It tantalized him that she should have such a loathing for him. He was used to being liked by women. It would be funny if one of these days she fell in love with him. He'd been her first lover and he'd heard the students in Munich over their beer saying that it was her first lover a woman loved, after that it was love. When he'd set his mind on getting a girl he'd never failed yet. Hans laughed to himself and a sly look came into his eyes.

The Unconquered

1 fancied 好きになる 2 full-breasted 胸の大きい fair-haired 金髪の 3 hefty and well-covered 大柄で、ちょっと太り気味の 4 refinement 上品さ account for 価値を置く 5 thin fine nose 小さくて形のいい鼻 6 intimidating たじろがせるような 8 and yet しかし 9 elated 気持ちが高揚していた 10 would never have crossed his mind (仮定法) 彼の心をよぎることは決してなかっただろう 11 have anything to do with her 彼女に手を出す

12 fortnight 2週間 get away 軍務を抜ける 14 wolfed たいらげた 16 the moment his back was turned 彼が背中を向けた瞬間 set to 食べ始める 17 getting something for nothing ただで何かを手に入れる 21 quite a lot しょっちゅう tantalized 悩ませた 22 loathing 嫌悪 used to being liked 好かれることに慣れていた 23 one of these days 近いうちに 24 He'd been her first lover 彼が彼女の初体験の相手だった and he'd heard the students in Munich over their beer ミュンヘンの学生たちがビールを飲みながらいうのをきく 26 after that その後は it was love 女は愛を愛するようになる 28 sly ずるそうな

37

At last he got his chance to go to the farm. He got hold of cheese and butter, sugar, a tin of sausages, and some coffee, and set off on his motor-cycle. But that time he didn't see Annette. She and her father were at work in the fields. The old woman was in the yard and her face lit up when she saw the parcel he was bringing. She led him into the kitchen. Her hands trembled a little as she untied the string and when she saw what he had brought her eyes filled with tears.

'You're very good,' she said.

'May I sit down?' he asked politely.

'Of course.' She looked out of the window and Hans guessed that she wanted to make sure that Annette was not coming. 'Can I offer you a glass of wine.'

'I'd be glad of it.'

He was sharp enough to see that her greed for food had made her, if not friendly to him, at least willing to come to terms with him. That look out of the window made them almost fellow conspirators.

'Did you like the pork?' he asked.

'It was a treat.'

'I'll try to bring you some more next time I come. Did Annette like it?'

'She wouldn't touch a thing you'd left. She said she'd rather starve.'

'Silly.'

'That's what I said to her. As long as the food is there, I said, there's nothing to be gained by not eating it.'

They chatted quite amicably while Hans sipped his

The Unconquered

2 **a tin** 缶詰 5 **yard** 庭 6 **parcel** 包み 8 **untied the string** ひもをほどいた
16 **sharp** 目ざとい 18 **come to terms with him** うまく付き合う 19 **fellow conspirators** 共謀者
21 **treat** ごちそう
29 **amicably** 親しく **sipped** すすった

wine. He discovered that she was called Madame Périer. He asked her whether there were any other members of the family. She sighed. No, they'd had a son, but he'd been mobilized at the beginning of the war and he'd died. He hadn't been killed, he'd got pneumonia and died in the hospital at Nancy.

'I'm sorry,' said Hans.

'Perhaps he's better off than if he'd lived. He was like Annette in many ways. He could never have borne the shame of defeat.' She sighed again. 'Oh, my poor friend, we've been betrayed.'

'Why did you want to fight for the Poles? What were they to you?'

'You're right. If we had let your Hitler take Poland he would have left us alone.'

When Hans got up to go he said he would come again soon.

'I shan't forget the pork.'

Then Hans had a lucky break; he was given a job that took him twice a week to a town in the vicinity so that he was able to get to the farm much oftener. He took care never to come without bringing something. But he made no headway with Annette. Seeking to ingratiate himself with her, he used the simple wiles that he had discovered went down with women; but they only excited her derision. Thin-lipped and hard, she looked at him as though he were dirt. On more than one occasion she made him so angry that he would have liked to take her by the shoulders and shake the life out of her. Once

The Unconquered

1 **Périer** ペリエ 4 **mobilized** 動員される 5 **pneumonia** 肺炎
6 **Nancy** ナンシー（フランス北東部の町）
9 **could never have borne**（仮定法）決して耐えられなかったでしょう 10 **my poor friend** 相手に対する呼びかけ。poor にはあまり意味がない。
12 **Poles** ポーランド人
15 **have left us alone** 放っておいてくれた
18 **shan't forget the pork** 豚肉を持ってくるのを忘れないようにする
19 **lucky break** 幸運 20 **vicinity** 近所 23 **headway** 進展 **ingratiate** 気に入られるようにする 24 **wiles** 計画、たくらみ **he had discovered**（挿入句）彼の知っていた 25 **went down with women** 女の子をものにする 26 **derision** 嘲笑 **Thin-lipped and hard** 唇を結んでけわしい顔で 27 **On more than one occasion** 何度も 28 **take her by the shoulders** 彼女の肩をつかんで 29 **shake the life out of her** 揺すぶって殺す

he found her alone, and when she got up to go he barred her passage.

'Stop where you are. I want to talk to you.'

'Talk. I am a woman and defenceless.'

'What I want to say is this: for all I know I may be here for a long time. Things aren't going to get easier for you French, they're going to get harder. I can be useful to you. Why don't you be reasonable like your father and mother?'

It was true that old Périer had come round. You couldn't say that he was cordial, he was indeed cold and gruff, but he was civil. He had even asked Hans to bring him some tobacco, and when he wouldn't accept payment for it had thanked him. He was pleased to hear the news of Soissons and grabbed the paper that Hans brought him. Hans, a farmer's son, could talk about the farm as one who knew. It was a good farm, not too big and not too small, well watered, for a sizable brook ran through it, and well wooded, with arable land and pasture. Hans listened with understanding sympathy when the old man bewailed himself because without labour, without fertilizers, his stock taken from him, it was all going to rack and ruin.

'You ask me why I can't be reasonable like my father and mother,' said Annette.

She pulled her dress tight and showed herself to him. He couldn't believe his eyes. What he saw caused such a convulsion in his soul as he had never known. The blood rushed to his cheeks.

The Unconquered

1 **barred her passage** 前に立ちふさがった
5 **for all I know**「自分の知る限り、たぶん」という意味だが、ここはただ遠回しにいっているだけ 8 **reasonable** 理性的、物わかりがいい
10 **had come round** 態度を和らげた **You**（一般人称） 11 **cordial** 温かく接してくれる 12 **gruff** ぶっきらぼう **civil** 礼儀正しい 13 **accept payment for it** 金をもらう **had thanked him** 彼に礼をいった 17 **knew**（あとに the farm が省略されている） 18 **sizable** 大きい **brook** 小川 19 **well wooded** 木がたくさん生えている **arable** 耕作に適した **pasture** 牧草地 21 **bewailed himself** 我が身を嘆いた 22 **fertilizers** 肥料 **stock** 家畜 **it** 一般的な状況 23 **rack and ruin** どうしようもない
26 **She pulled her dress tight and showed herself to him** 服をぴったり体に貼りつけるようにして、彼に見せた 27 **What he saw** 彼が見たもの 28 **convulsion** 激変

'You're pregnant.'

She sank back on her chair and leaning her head on her hands began to weep as though her heart would break.

'The shame of it. The shame.'

He sprang towards her to take her in his arms.

'My sweet,' he cried.

But she sprang to her feet and pushed him away.

'Don't touch me. Go away. Go away. Haven't you done me enough harm already?'

She flung out of the room. He waited by himself for a few minutes. He was bewildered. His thoughts in a whirl, he rode slowly back to Soissons, and when he went to bed he couldn't get to sleep for hours. He could think of nothing but Annette and her swollen body. She had been unbearably pathetic as she sat there at the table crying her eyes out. It was his child she bore in her womb. He began to feel drowsy, and then with a start he was once more wide awake, for suddenly it came to him, it came to him with the shattering suddenness of gun-fire: he was in love with her. It was such a surprise, such a shock that he couldn't cope with it. Of course he'd thought of her a lot, but never in that way, he'd thought it would be a great joke if he made her fall in love with him, it would be a triumph if the time came when she offered what he had taken by force; but not for a moment had it occurred to him that she was anything to him but a woman like another. She wasn't his type. She wasn't very pretty. There was nothing to her.

5 **The shame of it** 恥ずかしくてたまらない
8 **sprang to her feet** ぱっと立ち上がった
11 **flung out of the room** 部屋から駆けだした 12 **in a whirl** 渦巻いている 15 **but** (=except) **swollen** お腹のふくれた 16 **unbearably** 耐えがたく **pathetic** あわれな 17 **crying her eyes out** 目玉が飛びだすほど泣く（激しく泣く） 18 **drowsy** 眠い **with a start** はっとして 19 **for** というのは 20 **with the shattering suddenness** いきなり、突然 **of gun-fire** 銃火のように 22 **cope with** 処理する 23 **in that way** そんなふうに 26 **offered** 自分から捧げる **what he had taken by force** 自分が無理やり奪ったもの 27 **it occurred to him** 彼の頭に浮かんだ 28 **another** (=another woman)

Why should he have all of a sudden this funny feeling for her? It wasn't a pleasant feeling either, it was a pain. But he knew what it was all right; it was love, and it made him feel happier than he had ever felt in his life. He wanted to take her in his arms, he wanted to pet her, he wanted to kiss those tear-stained eyes of hers. He didn't desire her, he thought, as a man desires a woman, he wanted to comfort her, wanted her to smile at him — strange, he had never seen her smile, he wanted to see her eyes — fine eyes they were, beautiful eyes — soft with tenderness.

For three days he could not leave Soissons and for three days, three days and three nights, he thought of Annette and the child she would bear. Then he was able to go to the farm. He wanted to see Madame Périer by herself, and luck was with him, for he met her on the road some way from the house. She had been gathering sticks in the wood and was going home with a great bundle on her back. He stopped his motor-cycle. He knew that the friendliness she showed him was due only to the provisions he brought with him, but he didn't care; it was enough that she was mannerly, and that she was prepared to be so as long as she could get something out of him. He told her he wanted to talk to her and asked her to put her bundle down. She did as he bade. It was a grey, cloudy day, but not cold.

'I know about Annette,' he said.

She started.

'How did you find out? She was set on your not

3 **what it was**（it は this funny feeling for her）それがなんなのか
all right ちゃんと　5 **pet** 愛撫する
14 **bear** 産む　**Then** そしてやがて　15 **see Madame Périer by herself** ペリエ夫人とふたりきりで会う　18 **sticks** 小枝
19 **bundle** 束　21 **due only to** 〜にふさわしいだけの　**provisions** 食料など　22 **it**（that 以下）　23 **so as long as** 〜である限り　26 **bade** 命じた
28 **started** びっくりした
29 **was set on your not knowing** あなたに知られないようにしていた

knowing.'

'She told me.'

'That was a pretty job of work you did that evening.'

'I didn't know. Why didn't you tell me sooner?'

She began to talk, not bitterly, not blaming him even, but as though it were a misfortune of nature, like a cow dying in giving birth to a calf or a sharp spring frost nipping the fruit trees and ruining the crop, a misfortune that human kind must accept with resignation and humility. After that dreadful night Annette had been in bed for days with a high fever. They thought she was going out of her mind. She would scream for hours on end. There were no doctors to be got. The village doctor had been called to the colours. Even in Soissons there were only two doctors left, old men both of them, and how could they get to the farm even if it had been possible to send for them? They weren't allowed to leave the town. Even when the fever went down Annette was too ill to leave her bed, and when she got up she was so weak, so pale, it was pitiful. The shock had been terrible, and when a month went by, and another month, without her being unwell she paid no attention. She had always been irregular. It was Madame Périer who first suspected that something was wrong. She questioned Annette. They were terrified, both of them, but they weren't certain and they said nothing to Périer. When the third month came it was impossible to doubt any longer. Annette was pregnant.

They had an old Citroën in which before the war

3 **pretty job of work** 大変なこと
6 **a misfortune of nature** 天災　7 **calf** 子牛　8 **nipping** 凍えさせる、枯らす　**crop** 穀物　9 **resignation** あきらめ　**humility** 謙虚さ　10 **After that**（ここからは母親の語ったこと）　11 **going out of her mind** 頭がおかしくなる　12 **on end** ずっと
14 **colours** 軍隊　17 **send for** 呼びにやる　22 **unwell** 生理中
23 **irregular** 生理が不順
29 **Citroën** シトロエン（フランス車）

Madame Périer had taken the farm produce into the market at Soissons two mornings a week, but since the German occupation they had had nothing to sell that made the journey worth while. Petrol was almost unobtainable. But now they got it out and drove into town. The only cars to be seen were the military cars of the Germans. German soldiers lounged about. There were German signs in the streets, and on public buildings proclamations in French signed by the Officer Commanding. Many shops were closed. They went to the old doctor they knew, and he confirmed their suspicions. But he was a devout Catholic and would not help them. When they wept he shrugged his shoulders.

'You're not the only one,' he said. '*Il faut souffrir.*'

They knew about the other doctor too and went to see him. They rang the bell and for a long time no one answered. At last the door was opened by a sad-faced woman in black, but when they asked to see the doctor she began to cry. He had been arrested by the Germans because he was a freemason, and was held as a hostage. A bomb had exploded in a café frequented by German officers and two had been killed and several wounded. If the guilty were not handed over before a certain date he was to be shot. The woman seemed kindly and Madame Périer told her of their trouble.

'The brutes,' she said. She looked at Annette with compassion. 'My poor child.'

She gave them the address of a midwife in the town and told them to say that they had come from her. The

The Unconquered

1 **farm produce** 畑でとれたもの　3 **occupation** 占領　4 **made the journey worth while** 車で売りに行くだけの価値のある　**Petrol** ガソリン　**unobtainable** 手に入らない　5 **got it out** (itは車) それを外に出して　7 **lounged** ぶらついていた　8 **German signs** ドイツ語の標識　9 **proclamations** 布告　**Officer Commanding** 司令官　11 **confirmed their suspicions** ふたりが疑っている通りだといった　12 **devout** 敬虔な

14 **Il faut souffrir** 苦しまなくてはなりません、耐えなくてはなりません

18 **in black** 喪服を着た　20 **freemason** フリーメーソン（イギリスで誕生した博愛主義団体）の会員（当時、ナチスの弾圧を受けていた）　**hostage** 人質　21 **frequented by German officers** ドイツ軍将校がよく足を運んでいた　23 **the guilty** 犯人たち　**handed over** 引き渡される　**a certain date** 決められたとき

26 **brutes** 獣（ドイツ軍を指している）

28 **midwife** 産婆

51

midwife gave them some medicine. It made Annette so ill that she thought she was going to die, but it had no further effect. Annette was still pregnant.

That was the story that Madame Périer told Hans. For a while he was silent.

'It's Sunday tomorrow,' he said then. 'I shall have nothing to do. I'll come and we'll talk. I'll bring something nice.'

'We have no needles. Can you bring some?'

'I'll try.'

She hoisted the bundle of sticks on her back and trudged down the road. Hans went back to Soissons. He dared not use his motor-cycle, so next day he hired a push-bike. He tied his parcel of food on the carrier. It was a larger parcel than usual because he had put a bottle of champagne into it. He got to the farm when the gathering darkness made it certain that they would all be home from work. It was warm and cosy in the kitchen when he walked in. Madame Périer was cooking and her husband was reading a *Paris-Soir*. Annette was darning stockings.

'Look, I've brought you some needles,' he said, as he undid his parcel. 'And here's some material for you, Annette.'

'I don't want it.'

'Don't you?' he grinned. 'You'll have to begin making things for the baby.'

'That's true, Annette,' said her mother, 'and we have nothing.' Annette did not look up from her sewing.

2 **had no further effect** それ以上の効き目はなかった
11 **hoisted** 背負い上げる　12 **trudged** とぼとぼ歩いた
13 **dared not** (=could not)　**hired** 借りた　14 **push-bike** 自転車
parcel 包み　**carrier** 乗り物（自転車）　16 **the gathering darkness** 濃くなっていく宵闇　18 **cosy** 気持ちがいい　20 **Paris-Soir**「パリ・ソワール」（新聞）　**darning** 繕っていた
23 **undid** 包みをほどく　**material** 生地

Madame Périer's greedy eyes ran over the contents of the parcel. 'A bottle of champagne.'

Hans chuckled.

'I'll tell you what that's for presently. I've had an idea.' He hesitated for a moment, then drew up a chair and sat down facing Annette. 'I don't know quite how to begin. I'm sorry for what I did that night, Annette. It wasn't my fault, it was the circumstances. Can't you forgive me?'

She threw him a look of hatred.

'Never. Why don't you leave me alone? Isn't it enough that you've ruined my life?'

'Well, that's just it. Perhaps I haven't. When I knew you were going to have a baby it had a funny effect on me. It's all different now. It's made me so proud.'

'Proud?' she flung at him viciously.

'I want you to have the baby, Annette. I'm glad you couldn't get rid of it.'

'How dare you say that?'

'But listen to me. I've been thinking of nothing else since I knew. The war will be over in six months. We shall bring the English to their knees in the spring. They haven't got a chance. And then I shall be demobilized and I'll marry you.'

'You? Why?'

He blushed under his tan. He could not bring himself to say it in French, so he said it in German. He knew she understood it.

'*Ich liebe dich.*'

4 **I'll tell you** きみに教えてあげよう　**what that's for** これがなんのためのものか　**presently** すぐに　6 **how to begin** どう切り出していいか　8 **It wasn't my fault** 自分のせいじゃなかった　**circumstances** 状況

11 **leave me alone** 放っておく

13 **that's just it** まさにそこなんだ　**I haven't** (=I haven't ruined your life)

16 **flung** 視線を投げた　**viciously** 憎々しげな表情で、悪意をこめて

18 **get rid of it** (it は赤ん坊) その子を始末する

21 **in six months** (in は「後」) 6 カ月後　22 **bring the English to their knees** イギリス人をひざまずかせる　23 **be demobilized** 復員してドイツに帰される

26 **blushed** 顔を赤らめた　**tan** 日焼けした肌

29 **Ich liebe dich** (=I love you)

'What does he say?' asked Madame Périer.

'He says he loves me.'

Annette threw back her head and broke into a peal of harsh laughter. She laughed louder and louder and she couldn't stop and tears streamed from her eyes. Madame Périer slapped her sharply on both cheeks.

'Don't pay any attention,' she said to Hans. 'It's hysteria. Her condition, you know.'

Annette gasped. She gained control over herself.

'I brought the bottle of champagne to celebrate our engagement,' said Hans.

'That's the bitterest thing of all,' said Annette, 'that we were beaten by fools, by such fools.'

Hans went on speaking in German.

'I didn't know I loved you till that day when I found out that you were going to have a baby. It came like a clap of thunder, but I think I've loved you all the time.'

'What does he say?' asked Madame Périer.

'Nothing of importance.'

He fell back into French. He wanted Annette's parents to hear what he had to say.

'I'd marry you now, only they wouldn't let me. And don't think I'm nothing at all. My father's well-to-do and we're well thought of in our commune. I'm the eldest son and you'd want for nothing.'

'Are you a Catholic?' asked Madame Périer.

'Yes, I'm a Catholic.'

'That's something.'

'It's pretty, the country where we live and the soil's

3 **threw back her head** 頭をのけぞらせた **a peal of harsh laughter** 耳障りな声を張りあげて笑うこと
7 **Don't pay any attention** 気にしないでください **hysteria** ヒステリー
9 **gasped** あえいだ
12 **bitterest thing** いやでたまらないこと 13 **beaten** 打ち負かされる
17 **clap of thunder** 雷鳴
19 **Nothing of importance** どうでもいいこと
22 **I'd marry you now**（仮定法）できることなら、今すぐにでもきみと結婚したい **they wouldn't let me**（they は軍隊）そうさせてくれないだろう（結婚させてくれないだろう） 23 **I'm nothing at all** 能無し、でくのぼう **well-to-do** 金持ち 24 **well thought of** よく思われている **commune** 村 25 **want for nothing** 不自由なく暮らす
28 **That's something** それはありがたい、よかった
29 **It**（the country のこと） **the country** 田舎 **soil** 土地、土壌

good. There's not better farming land between Munich and Innsbruck, and it's our own. My grandfather bought it after the war of '70. And we've got a car and a radio, and we're on the telephone.'

Annette turned to her father.

'He has all the tact in the world, this gentleman,' she cried ironically. She eyed Hans. 'It would be a nice position for me, the foreigner from the conquered country with a child born out of wedlock. It offers me a chance of happiness, doesn't it? A fine chance.'

Périer, a man of few words, spoke for the first time.

'No. I don't deny that it's a fine gesture you're making. I went through the last war and we all did things we wouldn't have done in peace time. Human nature is human nature. But now that our son is dead, Annette is all we have. We can't let her go.'

'I thought you might feel that way,' said Hans, 'and I've got my answer to that. I'll stay here.'

Annette gave him a quick look.

'What do you mean?' asked Madame Périer.

'I've got another brother. He can stay and help my father. I like this country. With energy and initiative a man could make a good thing of your farm. When the war's over a lot of Germans will be settling here. It's well known that you haven't got enough men in France to work the land you've got. A fellow gave us a lecture the other day at Soissons. He said that a third of the farms were left uncultivated because there aren't the men to work them.'

The Unconquered

1 **There's not better farming land** そこ以上に良質な農地はない 2 **Innsbruck** インスブルック（オーストリア西部の市） 3 **the war of '70** 1870年の普仏戦争、プロイセン・フランス戦争（プロイセンが大勝利を収め、これを機にドイツ統一がなされ、1871年、ドイツ帝国が成立する）
6 **tact** 機転、如才なさ 7 **eyed** 見た **position** 地位 9 **a child born out of wedlock** 未婚の母から生まれた子
12 **gesture** 意思表示
19 **gave him a quick look** 彼をちらっと見た
22 **initiative** 才能、能力 23 **make a good thing of your farm** あなたがたの農場を素晴らしいものにする 24 **settling** 移り住む

Périer and his wife exchanged glances and Annette saw that they were wavering. That was what they'd wanted since their son had died, a son-in-law who was strong and hefty and could take over when they grew too old to do more than potter about.

'That changes the case,' said Madame Périer. 'It's a proposition to consider.'

'Hold your tongue,' cried Annette roughly. She leant forward and fixed her burning eyes on the German. 'I'm engaged to a teacher who worked in the boys' school in the town where I taught, we were to be married after the war. He's not strong and big like you, or handsome; he's small and frail. His only beauty is the intelligence that shines in his face, his only strength is the greatness of his soul. He's not a barbarian, he's civilized; he has a thousand years of civilization behind him. I love him. I love him with all my heart and soul.'

Hans's face grew sullen. It had never occurred to him that Annette might care for anyone else.

'Where is he now?'

'Where do you suppose he is? In Germany. A prisoner and starving. While you eat the fat of our land. How many times have I got to tell you that I hate you? You ask me to forgive you. Never. You want to make reparation. You fool.' She threw her head back and there was a look of intolerable anguish on her face. 'Ruined. Oh, he'll forgive me. He's tender. But I'm tortured by the thought that one day the suspicion may come to him that perhaps I hadn't been forced — that perhaps I'd given

2 **wavering** 心が揺れる　4 **hefty** 屈強な　5 **potter** ぶらぶらする
6 **That changes the case** それなら話は別ね
8 **Hold your tongue** 黙ってちょうだい　13 **frail** 虚弱な
15 **barbarian** 野蛮人
18 **sullen** 不機嫌　19 **care for** 好き
21 **Where do you suppose he is?** (do you suppose は挿入句) 彼がどこにいると思う？　24 **reparation** 償い　26 **intolerable** 耐えがたい　**anguish** 苦悶　**Ruined** (I'm ruined) わたしは破滅した、もうだめ　29 **hadn't been forced** 無理やり犯されたのではない

myself to you for butter and cheese and silk stockings. I shouldn't be the only one. And what would our life be with that child between us, your child, a German child? Big like you, and blond like you, and blue-eyed like you. Oh, my God, why do I have to suffer this?'

She got up and went swiftly out of the kitchen. For a minute the three were left in silence. Hans looked ruefully at his bottle of champagne. He sighed and rose to his feet. When he went out Madame Périer accompanied him.

'Did you mean it when you said you would marry her?' she asked him, speaking in a low voice.

'Yes. Every word. I love her.'

'And you wouldn't take her away? You'd stay here and work on the farm?'

'I promise you.'

'Evidently my old man can't last for ever. At home you'd have to share with your brother. Here you'd share with nobody.'

'There's that too.'

'We never were in favour of Annette marrying that teacher, but our son was alive then and he said, if she wants to marry him, why shouldn't she? Annette was crazy about him. But now that our son's dead, poor boy, it's different. Even if she wanted to, how could she work the farm alone?'

'It would be a shame if it was sold. I know how one feels about one's own land.'

They had reached the road. She took his hand and

The Unconquered

2 **I shouldn't be the only one** 自分だけではないだろう（ほかにもそういうことをした女がいるだろう）
7 **ruefully** 悲しげに 8 **rose to his feet** 立ち上がった
11 **mean it** 本気だった
13 **Every word** ひと言残らず、すべて
17 **last** 生き続ける **At home** あなたの故郷では 18 **share with your brother** 弟さんとふたりで農場を分ける
20 **There's that too** その通りです
21 **never were in favour of** よいとは思っていなかった 24 **crazy** 夢中
27 **be a shame** もったいない

gave it a little squeeze.

'Come again soon.'

Hans knew that she was on his side. It was a comfort to him to think that as he rode back to Soissons. It was a bother that Annette was in love with somebody else. Fortunately he was a prisoner; long before he was likely to be released the baby would be born. That might change her: you could never tell with a woman. Why, in his village there'd been a woman who was so much in love with her husband that it had been a joke, and then she had a baby and after that she couldn't bear the sight of him. Well, why shouldn't the contrary happen too? And now that he'd offered to marry her she must see that he was a decent sort of fellow. God, how pathetic she'd looked with her head flung back, and how well she'd spoken! What language! An actress on the stage couldn't have expressed herself better, and yet it had all sounded so natural. You had to admit that, these French people knew how to talk. Oh, she was clever. Even when she lashed him with that bitter tongue it was a joy to listen to her. He hadn't had a bad education himself, but he couldn't hold a candle to her. Culture, that's what she had.

'I'm a donkey,' he said out loud as he rode along. She'd said he was big and strong and handsome. Would she have said that if it hadn't meant something to her? And she'd talked of the baby having fair hair and blue eyes like his own. If that didn't mean that his colouring had made an impression on her he was a Dutchman. He

1 **gave it a little squeeze** 手を軽く握った
5 **a bother** 気になること   7 **be released** 釈放される   8 **you could never tell with a woman** 女というのはわからないものだ   10 **it had been a joke** 冗談のネタになった   12 **him** (=her husband)   14 **decent** ちゃんとした、きちんとした **sort of** 多少は   15 **flung back** 頭をのけぞらせた   16 **An actress on the stage couldn't have expressed herself better** 舞台の女優だって、あれほど雄弁に自分を表現することはできなかっただろう   17 **and yet** それでいて   18 **You** (一般人称)   20 **lashed** むち打つ   22 **couldn't hold a candle to** ～とくらべると劣る
24 **donkey** ロバ、田舎者   26 **if it hadn't meant something to her** (仮定法) 彼女にとって好ましいことでなかったら   27 **fair hair** 金髪   28 **If that didn't mean that his colouring had made an impression on her** もしそのこと（彼女が、赤ん坊は彼のように金髪で青い瞳だろうといったこと）が、彼の特徴が彼女になんらかの影響を与えているということを意味していないとしたら→彼女が、赤ん坊は金髪で青い瞳だろうといったのが、おれに気があるという証拠でなかったとしたら   29 **he was a Dutchman** (決まり文句で) いや、そんなことは絶対にない

chuckled. 'Give me time. Patience, and let nature go to work.'

The weeks went by. The CO at Soissons was an elderly, easy-going fellow and in view of what the spring had in store for them he was content not to drive his men too hard. The German papers told them that England was being wrecked by the Luftwaffe and the people were in a panic. Submarines were sinking British ships by the score and the country was starving. Revolution was imminent. Before summer it would be all over and the Germans would be masters of the world. Hans wrote home and told his parents that he was going to marry a French girl and with her a fine farm. He proposed that his brother should borrow money to buy him out of his share of the family property so that he could increase the size of his own holding while land, owing to the war and the exchange, could still be bought for a song. He went over the farm with Périer. The old man listened quietly when Hans told him his ideas: the farm would have to be restocked and as a German he would have a pull; the motor tractor was old, he would get a fine new one from Germany, and a motor plough. To make a farm pay you had to take advantage of modern inventions. Madame Périer told him afterwards that her husband had said he wasn't a bad lad and seemed to know a lot. She was very friendly with him now and insisted that he should share their midday meal with them on Sundays. She translated his name into French and called him Jean. He was always ready to give a hand, and as time

The Unconquered

1 **Patience** 忍耐　**let nature go to work** 本性、自然に働いてもらおう
3 **CO**（commanding officer）司令官、部隊長　4 **in view of** 〜を考慮して　**what the spring had in store** 春が用意してくれたもの　5 **drive his men too hard** 部下を激しく働かせる　7 **wrecked** 壊滅状態　**Luftwaffe** ドイツ空軍　9 **by the score**（score は 20 の意味）20 隻単位で（次々に）　10 **imminent** 迫っている　11 **wrote home** 故郷に（家族に）手紙を書いた　13 **with her a fine farm** 彼女には素晴らしい畑がついてくる　14 **him**（弟）　**out of his share of the family property** 財産の彼の取り分を前借りして　16 **holding** 自分の土地　**owing to** 〜のおかげで　17 **exchange** 為替相場　**for a song** 二束三文で　20 **be restocked** 新たに買う　21 **pull** コネ　22 **motor plough** 耕運機　**To make a farm pay** 畑にもうけさせるためには　23 **take advantage of** 利用する　**inventions** 新しい機械　25 **lad** 男　**know a lot** よく知っている、経験が豊富な　27 **midday meal** 昼食　29 **Jean** ジャン　**give a hand** 手を差しだす、手助けをする

went on and Annette could do less and less it was useful to have a man about who didn't mind doing a job of work.

Annette remained fiercely hostile. She never spoke to him except to answer his direct questions and as soon as it was possible went to her own room. When it was so cold that she couldn't stay there she sat by the side of the kitchen stove, sewing or reading, and took no more notice of him than if he hadn't been there. She was in radiant health. There was colour in her cheeks and in Hans's eyes she was beautiful. Her approaching maternity had given her a strange dignity and he was filled with exultation when he gazed upon her. Then one day when he was on his way to the farm he saw Madame Périer in the road waving to him to stop. He put his brakes on hard.

'I've been waiting for an hour. I thought you'd never come. You must go back. Pierre is dead.'

'Who's Pierre?'

'Pierre Gavin. The teacher Annette was going to marry.'

Hans's heart leapt. What luck! Now he'd have his chance.

'Is she upset?'

'She's not crying. When I tried to say something she bit my head off. If she saw you today she's capable of sticking a knife into you.'

'It's not my fault if he died. How did you hear?'

'A prisoner, a friend of his, escaped through Switz-

The Unconquered

1 **Annette could do less and less** いろんなことができなくなってくる 2 **about** 近くに **mind** いやがる **doing a job of work** 仕事をすること

8 **took no more notice of him than if he hadn't been there** 彼がそこにいないのと同じような態度を取った 10 **radiant** 申し分のない 11 **approaching** 近づいてくる **maternity** 母親になること 13 **exultation** 大きな喜び 15 **put his brakes on hard** 思いきりブレーキをかけた

26 **bit my head off** わたしの首を嚙みきった（くってかかった）

28 **How did you hear?** どんなことをきいたのですか？

erland and he wrote to Annette. We got the letter this morning. There was a mutiny in the camp because they weren't given enough to eat, and the ringleaders were shot. Pierre was one of them.'

Hans was silent. He could only think it served the man right. What did they think that a prison camp was — the Ritz?

'Give her time to get over the shock,' said Madame Périer. 'When she's calmer I'll talk to her. I'll write you a letter when you can come again.'

'All right. You will help me, won't you?'

'You can be sure of that. My husband and I, we're agreed. We talked it over and we came to the conclusion that the only thing to do was to accept the situation. He's no fool, my husband, and he says the best chance for France now is to collaborate. And take it all in all I don't dislike you. I shouldn't wonder if you didn't make Annette a better husband than that teacher. And with the baby coming and all.'

'I want it to be a boy,' said Hans.

'It's going to be a boy. I know for certain. I've seen it in the coffee grounds and I've put out the cards. The answer is a boy every time.'

'I almost forgot, here are some papers for you,' said Hans, as he turned his cycle and prepared to mount.

He handed her three numbers of *Paris-Soir*. Old Périer read every evening. He read that the French must be realistic and accept the new order that Hitler was going to create in Europe. He read that the German submarines

The Unconquered

2 **mutiny** 反乱、騒動 **the camp** 収容所 3 **ringleaders** 首謀者 5 **it served the man right** 当然の報いだった 6 **What did they think that a prison camp was** やつらは収容所をなんだと考えていたのか 7 **Ritz** リッツ（高級ホテル）

12 **can be sure of that** それに関しては信用してもらっていい

16 **collaborate** 協力する **take it all in all** いろいろあったけれど 17 **shouldn't wonder** 不思議に思わない **make Annette a better husband than that teacher** アネットにとって、あの教師（婚約者）よりいい夫になる 18 **with the baby coming and all** 赤ん坊も生まれるし

22 **coffee grounds** コーヒーの出しがら（出しがらの模様で占う） **put out the cards** トランプでも占ってみた

28 **the new order** 新しい秩序

were sweeping the sea. He read that the General Staff had organized to the last detail the campaign that would bring England to her knees and that the Americans were too unprepared, too soft and too divided to come to her help. He read that France must take the heaven-sent opportunity and by loyal collaboration with the Reich regain her honoured position in the new Europe. And it wasn't Germans who wrote it all; it was Frenchmen. He nodded his head with approval when he read that the plutocrats and the Jews would be destroyed and the poor man in France would at last come into his own. They were quite right, the clever fellows who said that France was essentially an agricultural country and its backbone was its industrious farmers. Good sense, that was.

One evening, when they were finishing their supper, ten days after the news had come of Pierre Gavin's death, Madame Périer, by arrangement with her husband, said to Annette:

'I wrote a letter to Hans a few days ago telling him to come here tomorrow.'

'Thank you for the warning. I shall stay in my room.'

'Oh, come, daughter, the time has passed for foolishness. You must be realistic. Pierre is dead. Hans loves you and wants to marry you. He's a fine-looking fellow. Any girl would be proud of him as a husband. How can we restock the farm without his help? He's going to buy a tractor and a plough with his own money. You must let bygones be bygones.'

'You're wasting your breath, Mother. I earned my liv-

The Unconquered

1 **sweeping** 堂々と航行する　**General Staff** 参謀幕僚　2 **to the last detail** 最後の細かいところまで　3 **bring England to her knees** イギリスをひざまずかせる　4 **soft** 軟弱　**divided** (国内世論が) 分かれている　5 **heaven-sent** 天来の、時宜を得た　6 **loyal collaboration** 信頼できる協力関係　**the Reich** ナチスドイツの国家　10 **plutocrats** 金権主義者　**Jews** ユダヤ人　11 **come into his own** 本来自分のものであるものを手に入れる

14 **Good sense** 良識

17 **by arrangement** あらかじめ打ち合わせておいて

26 **restock** 新たに耕作する　28 **bygones be bygones** 終わったことは終わったことにする (あきらめる)

29 **wasting your breath** 息 (言葉) を無駄にしている　**earned my living** 自分の生活費を稼いできた

ing before, I can earn my living again. I hate him. I hate his vanity and his arrogance. I could kill him: his death wouldn't satisfy me. I should like to torture him as he's tortured me. I think I should die happy if I could find a way to wound him as he's wounded me.'

'You're being very silly, my poor child.'

'Your mother's right, my girl,' said Périer. 'We've been defeated and we must accept the consequences. We've got to make the best arrangement we can with the conquerors. We're cleverer than they are and if we play our cards well we shall come out on top. France was rotten. It's the Jews and the plutocrats who ruined the country. Read the papers and you'll see for yourself!'

'Do you think I believe a word in that paper? Why do you think he brings it to you except that it's sold to the Germans? The men who write in it — traitors, traitors. Oh God, may I live to see them torn to pieces by the mob. Bought, bought every one of them — bought with German money. The swine.'

Madame Périer was getting exasperated.

'What have you got against the boy? He took you by force — yes, he was drunk at the time. It's not the first time that's happened to a woman and it won't be the last time. He hit your father and he bled like a pig, but does your father bear him malice?'

'It was an unpleasant incident, but I've forgotten it,' said Périer.

Annette burst into harsh laughter.

'You should have been a priest. You forgive injuries

2 **vanity** 虚栄心　**arrogance** 傲慢さ
9 **we can** われわれができるかぎりの　10 **play our cards well**（トランプなどでいい手を作る、うまく勝負を運ぶ）うまく立ち回る　11 **come out on top** 上に立つ、出し抜く　12 **plutocrats** 金権政治家
15 **except that** that 以下の理由以外で　16 **traitors** 裏切り者　17 **may I live**（may は祈願を表す）生きられますように
18 **bought every one of them** あの人たち（The men who write in it）はひとり残らず買収されている　19 **swine** 豚
20 **exasperated** かっとなる、激怒する
21 **What have you got against the boy?** あの青年のどこがいやなの？　22 **It's not the first time that's happened to a woman** 女があなたのような目に合うのはこれが初めてじゃない
24 **bled** 血を流した　25 **bear him malice** うらみを抱く

with a spirit truly Christian.'

'And what is there wrong about that?' asked Madame Périer angrily. 'Hasn't he done everything he could to make amends? Where would your father have got his tobacco all these months if it hadn't been for him? If we haven't gone hungry it's owing to him.'

'If you'd had any pride, if you'd had any sense of decency, you'd have thrown his presents in his face.'

'You've profited by them, haven't you?'

'Never. Never.'

'It's a lie and you know it. You've refused to eat the cheese he brought and the butter and the sardines. But the soup you've eaten, you know I put the meat in it that he brought; and the salad you ate tonight, if you didn't have to eat it dry, it's because he brought me oil.'

Annette sighed deeply. She passed her hand over her eyes.

'I know. I tried not to, I couldn't help myself, I was so hungry. Yes, I knew his meat went into the soup and I ate it. I knew the salad was made with his oil. I wanted to refuse it; I had such a longing for it, it wasn't I that ate it, it was a ravenous beast within me.'

'That's neither here nor there. You ate it.'

'With shame. With despair. They broke our strength first with their tanks and their planes, and now when we're defenceless they're breaking our spirit by starving us.'

'You get nowhere by being theatrical, my girl. For an educated woman you have really no sense. Forget the

1 **a spirit truly Christian** じつにキリスト教徒的な精神（皮肉でいっている）
4 **make amends** 償いをする　5 **if it hadn't been for him**（仮定法）彼がいなかったら
7 **decency** 人間としての誇り
9 **You've profited by them** あなただって彼の持ってくる物の恩恵を受けてきた
15 **eat it dry** ドレッシングなしで食べる
22 **ravenous** 貪欲な
23 **That's neither here nor there** 取るに足りない
28 **get nowhere** どこにも行きつかない、無駄だ　**theatrical** 大げさな

past and give a father to your child, to say nothing of a good workman for the farm who'll be worth two hired men. That is sense.'

Annette shrugged her shoulders wearily and they lapsed into silence. Next day Hans came. Annette gave him a sullen look, but neither spoke nor moved. Hans smiled.

'Thank you for not running away,' he said.

'My parents asked you to come and they've gone down to the village. It suits me because I want to have a definite talk with you. Sit down.'

He took off his coat and his helmet and drew a chair to the table.

'My parents want me to marry you. You've been clever; with your presents, with your promises, you've got round them. They believe all they read in the papers you bring them. I want to tell you that I will never marry you. I wouldn't have thought it possible that I could hate a human being as I hate you.'

'Let me speak in German. You understand enough to know what I'm saying.'

'I ought to. I taught it. For two years I was governess to two little girls in Stuttgart.'

He broke into German, but she went on speaking French.

'It's not only that I love you, I admire you. I admire your distinction and your grace. There's something about you I don't understand. I respect you. Oh, I can see that you don't want to marry me now even if it were

1 **to say nothing of** いうまでもなく　3 **sense** 分別
4 **wearily** 疲れ切った様子で　5 **lapsed into silence** ふっと黙りこんでしまった　6 **sullen look** 不機嫌な表情　**nor moved** 身動きもしなかった
10 **It suits me** 自分にちょうどいい　11 **definite talk** はっきりした話
16 **got round** 言いくるめた
22 **ought to**（=ought to understand）　**governess** 住みこみの家庭教師　23 **Stuttgart** シュトゥットガルト（ドイツ南西部の都市）
27 **distinction** 非凡さ、気品、個性

possible. But Pierre is dead.'

'Don't speak of him,' she cried violently. 'That would be the last straw.'

'I only want to tell you that for your sake I'm sorry he died.'

'Shot in cold blood by his German jailers.'

'Perhaps in time you'll grieve for him less. You know, when someone you love dies, you think you'll never get over it, but you do. Won't it be better then to have a father for your child?'

'Even if there were nothing else do you think I could ever forget that you are a German and I'm a Frenchwoman? If you weren't as stupid as only a German can be you'd see that that child must be a reproach to me as long as I live. Do you think I have no friends? How could I ever look them in the face with the child I had with a German soldier? There's only one thing I ask you; leave me alone with my disgrace. Go, go — for God's sake go and never come again.'

'But he's my child too. I want him.'

'You?' she cried in astonishment. 'What can a by-blow that you got in a moment of savage drunkenness mean to you?'

'You don't understand. I'm so proud and so happy. It was when I knew you were going to have a baby that I knew I loved you. At first I couldn't believe it; it was such a surprise to me. Don't you see what I mean? That child that's going to be born means everything in the world to me. Oh, I don't know how to put it; it's put

3 **the last straw** 最後の一押し（It's the last straw that breaks the camel's back.「ワラの最後の一本がラクダの背骨を折る」という諺から。つまり、「負担や我慢や忍耐の限界を超させる最後のわずかなもののこと。この場合、アネットは我慢に我慢を重ねているわけで、そこで彼のことを持ち出されると、どうなるかわからない、ということ）

6 **Shot in cold blood** 冷酷に殺された　**jailers** 収容所の看守

7 **in time** そのうち　**grieve** 悲しむ　8 **get over** 乗りこえる

13 **weren't as stupid as only a German can be** ドイツ人しかなれないほどの愚か者でなかったら　14 **a reproach** 恥辱

16 **in the face** 面と向かう　18 **disgrace** 屈辱

21 **by-blow** 私生児　22 **that you got in a moment of savage drunkenness** あなたが乱暴な酔っぱらいになっているときにはらませた

24 **It was when I knew you were going to have a baby that I knew I loved you**（It was...that の強調構文）自分がきみを愛していると知ったのは、きみが身ごもっているということを知ったときだったんだ　29 **put it** いう

feeling in my heart that I don't understand myself.'

She looked at him intently and there was a strange gleam in her eyes. You would have said it was a look of triumph. She gave a short laugh.

'I don't know whether I more loathe the brutality of you Germans or despise your sentimentality.'

He seemed not to have heard what she said.

'I think of him all the time.'

'You've made up your mind it'll be a boy?'

'I know it'll be a boy. I want to hold him in my arms and I want to teach him to walk. And then when he grows older I'll teach him all I know. I'll teach him to ride and I'll teach him to shoot. Are there fish in your brook? I'll teach him to fish. I'm going to be the proudest father in the world.'

She stared at him with hard, hard eyes. Her face was set and stern. An idea, a terrible idea was forming itself in her mind.

He gave her a disarming smile.

'Perhaps when you see how much I love our boy, you'll come to love me too. I'll make you a good husband, my pretty.'

She said nothing. She merely kept on gazing at him sullenly.

'Haven't you one kind word for me?' he said.

She flushed. She clasped her hands tightly together.

'Others may despise me. I will never do anything that can make me despise myself. You are my enemy and you will always be my enemy. I only live to see

The Unconquered

2 **intently** 真剣に　3 **You**（一般人称）
5 **loathe** 心底嫌う　6 **sentimentality** 感傷的なところ
14 **brook** 小川
16 **hard eyes** きつい目　17 **set** 固い　**stern** 厳しい
19 **disarming** 安心させるような
21 **make you a good husband** きみのいい夫になる　22 **my pretty**（相手に対する呼びかけ）
24 **sullenly** むっつりして
26 **clasped** 組んだ

the deliverance of France. It'll come, perhaps not next year or the year after, perhaps not for thirty years, but it'll come. The rest of them can do what they like, I will never come to terms with the invaders of my country. I hate you and I hate this child that you've given me. Yes, we've been defeated. Before the end comes you'll see that we haven't been conquered. Now go. My mind's made up and nothing on God's earth can change it.'

He was silent for a minute or two.

'Have you made arrangements for a doctor? I'll pay all the expenses.'

'Do you suppose we want to spread our shame through the whole countryside? My mother will do all that's necessary.'

'But supposing there's an accident?'

'And supposing you mind your own business!'

He sighed and rose to his feet. When he closed the door behind him she watched him walk down the pathway that led to the road. She realized with rage that some of the things he said had aroused in her heart a feeling that she had never felt for him before.

'O God, give me strength,' she cried.

Then, as he walked along, the dog, an old dog they'd had for years, ran up to him barking angrily. He had tried for months to make friends with the dog, but it had never responded to his advances; when he tried to pat it, it backed away growling and showing its teeth. And now as the dog ran towards him, irritably giving way to his feeling of frustration, Hans gave it a savage brutal

1 deliverance 解放　3 The rest of them ほかの人たち　4 come to terms あきらめて付き合う　6 Before the end comes 終わりがくるまえに　7 My mind's made up わたしの心は決まっている　8 on God's earth（強調）

13 countryside 田舎、地方

18 pathway 小道

26 advances 懐柔　pat 軽くたたいてやる　27 backed away 後ずさった　28 irritably いらだって　giving way to his feeling of frustration むしゃくしゃしてたまらない気持ちに負けて　29 savage 野蛮な　brutal 乱暴な

kick and the dog was flung into the bushes and limped yelping away.

'The beast,' she cried. 'Lies, lies, lies. And I was weak enough to be almost sorry for him.'

There was a looking-glass hanging by the side of the door and she looked at herself in it. She drew herself up and smiled at her reflection. But rather than a smile it was a fiendish grimace.

It was now March. There was a bustle of activity in the garrison at Soissons. There were inspections and there was intensive training. Rumour was rife. There was no doubt they were going somewhere, but the rank and file could only guess where. Some thought they were being got ready at last for the invasion of England, others were of opinion that they would be sent to the Balkans, and others again talked of the Ukraine. Hans was kept busy. It was not till the second Sunday afternoon that he was able to get out to the farm. It was a cold grey day, with sleet that looked as though it might turn to snow falling in sudden windy flurries. The country was grim and cheerless.

'You!' cried Madame Périer when he went in. 'We thought you were dead.'

'I couldn't come before. We're off any day now. We don't know when.'

'The baby was born this morning. It's a boy.'

Hans's heart gave a great leap in his breast. He hung his arms round the old woman and kissed her on both cheeks.

The Unconquered

1 **limped yelping away** キャンキャン吠えながら、足を引きずって逃げていった
5 **looking-glass** 姿見、大きな鏡　6 **drew herself up** 胸を張って立った　8 **fiendish** 悪魔のような　**grimace** しかめっ面
9 **bustle of activity** あわただしい動き　10 **garrison inspections** 視察　11 **intensive training** 集中訓練　**rife** 広まって　12 **rank and file** 兵隊たち　15 **were of opinion** that 以下のような意見だった　16 **Balkans** バルカン諸国（クロアチア、マケドニア、ルーマニア、ブルガリア、ギリシアなど）　**Ukraine** ウクライナ（現在はヨーロッパ東部の共和国だが、当時はソビエト連邦の一部で、第2次世界大戦ではドイツ軍に侵攻され、550万人の犠牲者が出た）　19 **sleet** みぞれ　20 **windy flurries** 激しい風
24 **We're off any day now** いつ出発するかわからない　**We don't know when** いつか、わからないんだ

'A Sunday child, he ought to be lucky. Let's open the bottle of champagne. How's Annette?'

'She's as well as can be expected. She had a very easy time. She began to have pains last night and by five o'clock this morning it was all over.'

Old Périer was smoking his pipe sitting as near the stove as he could get. He smiled quietly at the boy's enthusiasm.

'One's first child, it has an effect on one,' he said.

'He has quite a lot of hair and it's as fair as yours; and blue eyes just like you said he'd have,' said Madame Périer. 'I've never seen a lovelier baby. He'll be just like his papa.'

'Oh, my God, I'm so happy,' cried Hans. 'How beautiful the world is! I want to see Annette.'

'I don't know if she'll see you. I don't want to upset her on account of the milk.'

'No, no, don't upset her on my account. If she doesn't want to see me it doesn't matter. But let me see the baby just for a minute.'

'I'll see what I can do. I'll try to bring it down.'

Madame Périer went out and they heard her heavy tread clumping up the stairs. But in a moment they heard her clattering down again. She burst into the kitchen.

'They're not there. She isn't in her room. The baby's gone.'

Périer and Hans cried out and without thinking what they were doing all three of them scampered upstairs.

3 **as well as can be expected** とても具合がいい **had a very easy time** 安産だった
9 **has an effect on** 〜に影響を与える
17 **on account of the milk** 母乳が出なくなるといけないから
23 **tread** 足音 **clumping** ドシンドシンと音を立てる 24 **clattering down** 騒々しく下りてくる足音
29 **scampered upstairs** あわてて駆け上がった

The harsh light of the winter afternoon cast over the shabby furniture, the iron bed, the cheap wardrobe, the chest of drawers, a dismal squalor. There was no one in the room.

'Where is she?' screamed Madame Périer. She ran into the narrow passage, opening doors, and called the girl's name. 'Annette, Annette. Oh, what madness!'

'Perhaps in the sitting-room.'

They ran downstairs to the unused parlour. An icy air met them as they opened the door. They opened the door of a storeroom.

'She's gone out. Something awful has happened.'

'How could she have got out?' asked Hans sick with anxiety.

'Through the front door, you fool.'

Périer went up to it and looked.

'That's right. The bolt's drawn back.'

'Oh, my God, my God, what madness,' cried Madame périer. 'It'll kill her.'

'We must look for her,' said Hans. Instinctively, because that was the way he always went in and out, he ran back into the kitchen and the others followed him. 'Which way?'

'The brook,' the old woman gasped.

He stopped as though turned to stone with horror. He stared at the old woman aghast.

'I'm frightened,' she cried. 'I'm frightened.'

Hans flung open the door, and as he did so Annette walked in. She had nothing on but her nightdress and

2 **shabby** みすぼらしい　**wardrobe** ワードローブ（洋服だんす）
3 **chest of drawers** 整理だんす　**dismal** 陰気な　**squalor** みすぼらしさ
8 **sitting-room** 居間
9 **parlour** (=sitting-room)　11 **storeroom** 食料などの貯蔵室
13 **sick with anxiety** 不安で吐き気がする
17 **The bolt's drawn back** かんぬきが引き抜いてある
21 **that was the way he always went in and out** 彼があれこれするときのいつものやり方 (Instinctively)
24 **gasped** はっと息を飲む
25 **turned to stone with horror** 恐怖で石のようになってしまった　26 **aghast** おどおどと
29 **had nothing on** 何も着ていなかった　**but** 〜以外　**night-dress** 寝間着

a flimsy rayon dressing-gown. It was pink, with pale blue flowers. She was soaked, and her hair, dishevelled, clung damply to her head and hung down her shoulders in bedraggled wisps. She was deathly white. Madame Périer sprang towards her and took her in her arms.

'Where have you been? Oh, my poor child, you're wet through. What madness!'

But Annette pushed her away. She looked at Hans.

'You've come at the right moment, you.'

'Where's the baby?' cried Madame Périer.

'I had to do it at once. I was afraid if I waited I shouldn't have the courage.'

'Annette, what have you done?'

'I've done what I had to do. I took it down to the brook and held it under water till it was dead.'

Hans gave a great cry, the cry of an animal wounded to death; he covered his face with his hands, and staggering like a drunken man flung out of the door. Annette sank into a chair, and leaning her forehead on her two fists burst into passionate weeping.

The Unconquered

1 **flimsy** 薄い　**rayon dressing-gown** レーヨンの化粧着（寝間着の上に着る）　2 **soaked** ずぶ濡れ　**dishevelled** 乱れている　3 **damply** 濡れて　**hung down her shoulders** 肩から垂れている　4 **bedraggled wisps** びしょ濡れの束
7 **through** 完全に
9 **at the right moment** ちょうどいいときに
17 **staggering** よろける

Sanatorium

For the first six weeks that Ashenden was at the sanatorium he stayed in bed. He saw nobody but the doctor who visited him morning and evening, the nurses who looked after him, and the maid who brought him his meals. He had contracted tuberculosis of the lungs, and since at the time there were reasons that made it difficult for him to go to Switzerland the specialist he saw in London had sent him up to a sanatorium in the north of Scotland. At last the day came that he had been patiently looking forward to when the doctor told him he could get up; and in the afternoon his nurse, having helped him to dress, took him down to the veranda, placed cushions behind him, wrapped him up in rugs, and left him to enjoy the sun that was streaming down from a cloudless sky. It was mid-winter. The sanatorium stood on the top of a hill and from it you had a spacious view of the snow-clad country. There were people lying all along the veranda in deckchairs, some chatting with their neighbours and some reading. Every now and then one would have a fit of coughing and you noticed that at the end of it he looked anxiously at his handkerchief. Before the nurse left Ashenden she turned with a kind of professional briskness to the man who was lying in the next chair.

'I want to introduce Mr Ashenden to you,' she said. And then to Ashenden: 'This is Mr McLeod. He and Mr Campbell have been here longer than anyone else.'

On the other side of Ashenden was lying a pretty girl, with red hair and bright blue eyes; she had on no make-

1 **Ashenden** アシェンデン(モームの *Ashenden; or, The British Agent* という諜報部員を主人公にした連作短編集の主人公) **sanatorium** 結核の療養所　4 **maid** メイド　5 **contracted tuberculosis of the lungs** 肺結核にかかっていた　6 **since at the time** そのとき以来　7 **specialist** 専門医　9 **the day...when** (when 以下は the day にかかる)　10 **looking forward to** 心待ちにする　13 **rugs** 上掛け　16 **spacious** 広々とした　17 **snow-clad** 雪におおわれた　19 **Every now and then** ときどき　20 **fit** 発作　21 **anxiously** 不安そうに　23 **briskness** きびきびした様子

26 **McLeod** マクラウド　27 **Campbell** キャンベル
29 **had on no make-up** 化粧をしていなかった

up, but her lips were very red and the colour on her cheeks was high. It emphasized the astonishing whiteness of her skin. It was lovely even when you realized that its delicate texture was due to illness. She wore a fur coat and was wrapped up in rugs, so that you could see nothing of her body, but her face was extremely thin, so thin that it made her nose, which wasn't really large, look a trifle prominent. She gave Ashenden a friendly look, but did not speak, and Ashenden, feeling rather shy among all those strange people, waited to be spoken to.

'First time they've let you get up, is it?' said McLeod.

'Yes.'

'Where's your room?'

Ashenden told him.

'Small. I know every room in the place. I've been here for seventeen years. I've got the best room here and so I damned well ought to have. Campbell's been trying to get me out of it, he wants it himself, but I'm not going to budge; I've got a right to it, I came here six months before he did.'

McLeod, lying there, gave you the impression that he was immensely tall; his skin was stretched tight over his bones, his cheeks and temples hollow, so that you could see the formation of his skull under it; and in that emaciated face, with its great bony nose, the eyes were preternaturally large.

'Seventeen years is a long time,' said Ashenden, because he could think of nothing else to say.

2 **high** 赤らんでいる 3 **you**（一般人称） 4 **texture** 肌理
7 **which wasn't really large** 本当はそれほど大きくない 8 **trifle** ちょっと **prominent** 大きい
18 **damned well** まちがいなく **ought to have** 〜すべき
20 **budge** 譲歩する
23 **immensely** 非常に **stretched tight** ぴったり張りついていた 24 **hollow** くぼんでいる 25 **formation** 形 **skull** 頭蓋骨
26 **emaciated** やせた 27 **preternaturally** 異常なくらい

'Time passes very quickly. I like it here. At first, after a year or two, I went away in the summer, but I don't any more. It's my home now. I've got a brother and two sisters; but they're married and now they've got families; they don't want me. When you've been here a few years and you go back to ordinary life, you feel a bit out of it, you know. Your pals have gone their own ways and you've got nothing in common with them any more. It all seems an awful rush. Much ado about nothing, that's what it is. It's noisy and stuffy. No, one's better off here. I shan't stir again till they carry me out feet first in my coffin.'

The specialist had told Ashenden that if he took care of himself for a reasonable time he would get well, and he looked at McLeod with curiosity.

'What do you do with yourself all day long?' he asked.

'Do? Having TB is a whole-time job, my boy. There's my temperature to take and then I weigh myself. I don't hurry over my dressing. I have breakfast, I read the papers and go for a walk. Then I have my rest. I lunch and play bridge. I have another rest and then I dine. I play a bit more bridge and I go to bed. They've got quite a decent library here, we get all the new books, but I don't really have much time for reading. I talk to people. You meet all sorts here, you know. They come and they go. Sometimes they go because they think they're cured, but a lot of them come back, and sometimes they go because they die. I've seen a lot of people out and before I

1 **I like it here** ここが好きだ 7 **out of it** 居心地が悪い、疎外感を持つ 9 **rush** あわただしさ **Much ado about nothing** どうでもいいことに大騒ぎする 10 **that's what it is** まさにそうなのだ **noisy and stuffy** 騒々しくて退屈 **one's**（one は人、この場合はサナトリウムの患者） **better off** いっそう楽いっそう楽 11 **shan't**（=shall not） **stir** 移動する **carry me out** 私を連れ出す **feet first** 足から先に 12 **coffin** 棺桶
14 **reasonable time** そこそこの時間
16 **What do you do with yourself** 何をしていらっしゃるのですか
18 **TB**（=tuberculosis）結核 **whole-time job** 一日仕事 19 **temperature to take** 熱を計る 20 **hurry over my dressing** 大急ぎで着替える 22 **bridge** ブリッジ（4人で行うトランプのゲーム。向かい合わせの2人が組になる） 24 **decent** ちゃんとした 26 **all sorts** いろんな種類の人々 29 **out** 死ぬ

go I expect to see a lot more.'

The girl sitting on Ashenden's other side suddenly spoke.

'I should tell you that few persons can get a heartier laugh out of a hearse than Mr McLeod,' she said.

McLeod chuckled.

'I don't know about that, but it wouldn't be human nature if I didn't say to myself: Well, I'm just as glad it's him and not me they're taking for a ride.'

It occurred to him that Ashenden didn't know the pretty girl, so he introduced him.

'By the way, I don't think you've met Mr Ashenden — Miss Bishop. She's English, but not a bad girl.'

'How long have *you* been here?' asked Ashenden.

'Only two years. This is my last winter. Dr Lennox says I shall be all right in a few months and there's no reason why I shouldn't go home.'

'Silly, I call it,' said McLeod. 'Stay where you're well off, that's what I say.'

At that moment a man, leaning on a stick, came walking slowly along the veranda.

'Oh, look, there's Major Templeton,' said Miss Bishop, a smile lighting up her blue eyes; and then, as he came up:

'I'm glad to see you up again.'

'Oh, it was nothing. Only a bit of a cold. I'm quite all right now.'

The words were hardly out of his mouth when he began to cough. He leaned heavily on his stick. But when

1 **go** 死ぬ
4 **few persons can get a heartier laugh out of a hearse than Mr McLeod** マクラウドさんほど、霊柩車をみてうれしそうに笑う人はまずいない
7 **I don't know about that** それはどうか知らない **it wouldn't be human nature** それは人間の本性に反する 8 **if I didn't say to myself** もし心の中で次のようにいわないとしたら、 **I'm just as glad it's him and not me they're taking for a ride** 連中が車で連れて行くのが自分じゃなくてほかの人間でよかった
10 **It occurred to him** マクラウドはふと思った
12 **By the way** ところで
18 **I call it** いわせてもらえば **you're well off** のんびり暮らしている
22 **Major Templeton** テンプルトン少佐
25 **up** ベッドから出る
26 **it was nothing** なんてことありませんでしたよ **a bit of a cold** ちょっと風邪をひいただけです
28 **The words were hardly out of his mouth when he began to cough** その言葉が口から出終わらないうちに、咳きこみ始めた

the attack was over he smiled gaily.

'Can't get rid of this damned cough,' he said. 'Smoking too much. Dr Lennox says I ought to give it up, but it's no good — I can't.'

He was a tall fellow, good-looking in a slightly theatrical way, with a dusky, sallow face, fine very dark eyes, and a neat black moustache. He was wearing a fur coat with an astrakhan collar. His appearance was smart and perhaps a trifle showy. Miss Bishop made Ashenden known to him. Major Templeton said a few civil words in an easy, cordial way, and then asked the girl to go for a stroll with him; he had been ordered to walk to a certain place in the wood behind the sanatorium and back again. McLeod watched them as they sauntered off.

'I wonder if there's anything between those two,' he said. 'They do say Templeton was a devil with the girls before he got ill.'

'He doesn't look up to much in that line just now,' said Ashenden.

'You never can tell. I've seen a lot of rum things here in my day. I could tell you no end of stories if I wanted to.'

'You evidently do, so why don't you?'

McLeod grinned.

'Well, I'll tell you one. Three or four years ago there was a woman here who was pretty hot stuff. Her husband used to come and see her every other week-end, he was crazy about her, used to fly up from London; but Dr Lennox was pretty sure she was carrying on with some-

1 **attack** 咳の発作　**gaily** 陽気に
4 **it's no good** 役に立たない
5 **slightly** ちょっと　**theatrical** 大げさな　6 **dusky** 浅黒い
sallow 血色の悪い　**dark** 黒い　7 **neat** きちんと手入れされた　8 **astrakhan** アストラハン（ロシア南東部の地名）産のヒツジの黒い毛皮　**smart** きちんとした　9 **trifle showy** ちょっと派手な　10 **civil words** ていねいな言葉　11 **easy** 気楽な
cordial 温かい　12 **stroll** 散歩　13 **back again** もどってくる
14 **sauntered off** ぶらぶら歩いていった
16 **devil with the girls** 女に手が早い
18 **look up to much** だいそれたことをする　**in that line** その点で
20 **tell** わかる　**rum things** やっかいごと　21 **in my day** 若かった頃　**no end of stories** 尽きることのない話
23 **evidently do** まちがいなく、そうでしょう
26 **pretty hot stuff** とてもいい女　28 **fly up** 飛行機でくる
29 **carrying on** いちゃつく

body here, but he couldn't find out who. So one night when we'd all gone to bed he had a thin coat of paint put down just outside her room and next day he had everyone's slippers examined. Neat, wasn't it? The fellow whose slippers had paint on them got the push. Dr Lennox has to be particular, you know. He doesn't want the place to get a bad name.'

'How long has Templeton been here?'

'Three or four months. He's been in bed most of the time. He's for it all right. Ivy Bishop'll be a damned fool if she gets stuck on him. She's got a good chance of getting well. I've seen so many of them, you know, I can tell. When I look at a fellow I make up my mind at once whether he'll get well or whether he won't, and if he won't I can make a pretty shrewd guess how long he'll last. I'm very seldom mistaken. I give Templeton about two years myself.'

McLeod gave Ashenden a speculative look, and Ashenden, knowing what he was thinking, though he tried to be amused, could not help feeling somewhat concerned. There was a twinkle in McLeod's eyes. He plainly knew what was passing through Ashenden's mind.

'You'll get all right. I wouldn't have mentioned it if I hadn't been pretty sure of that. I don't want Dr Lennox to hoof me out for putting the fear of God into his bloody patients.'

Then Ashenden's nurse came to take him back to bed. Even though he had only sat out for an hour, he was

2 **had a thin coat of paint put down** 塗料を薄く塗っておいた   4 **Neat, wasn't it?** うまいやり方だろう？   5 **slippers had paint on them** 塗料のついたスリッパ   **got the push** 追い出された   6 **particular** 厳しい   7 **get a bad name** 悪いうわさが立つ

10 **for it all right** まちがいなく危ない   11 **gets stuck on him** 彼と仲よくなる   12 **so many of them** よくなった人をたくさん   13 **I can tell** 自分にはわかる   **make up my mind** 決める   15 **shrewd** 鋭い   16 **I give Templeton about two years myself** テンプルトンはあと2年くらいだと思う

18 **speculative** さぐるような   20 **be amused** 楽しんでいる   21 **concerned** 不安な   **twinkle** きらめき   22 **plainly** はっきりと   **what was passing through Ashenden's mind** アシェンデンの頭をよぎったこと

25 **that** (=You'll get all right.)   26 **hoof me out** 追い出す   **putting the fear of God into** ひどく怖がらせる   27 **bloody patients** (bloodyにはあまり意味はない) ここの患者たち

tired, and was glad to find himself once more between the sheets. Dr Lennox came in to see him in the course of the evening. He looked at his temperature chart.

'That's not so bad,' he said.

Dr Lennox was small, brisk, and genial. He was a good enough doctor, an excellent business man, and an enthusiastic fisherman. When the fishing season began he was inclined to leave the care of his patients to his assistants; the patients grumbled a little, but were glad enough to eat the young salmon he brought back to vary their meals. He was fond of talking, and now, standing at the end of Ashenden's bed, he asked him, in his broad Scots, whether he had got into conversation with any of the patients that afternoon. Ashenden told him the nurse had introduced him to McLeod. Dr Lennox laughed.

'The oldest living inhabitant. He knows more about the sanatorium and its inmates than I do. How he gets his information I haven't an idea, but there's not a thing about the private lives of anyone under this roof that he doesn't know. There's not an old maid in the place with a keener nose for a bit of scandal. Did he tell you about Campbell?'

'He mentioned him.'

'He hates Campbell, and Campbell hates him. Funny, when you come to think of it, those two men, they've been here for seventeen years and they've got about one sound lung between them. They loathe the sight of one another. I've had to refuse to listen to the complaints about one another that they come to me with. Camp-

1 **between the sheets** ベッドにもぐりこむ 2 **in the course of** ～の間に 3 **temperature chart** 体温をつけた表
5 **brisk** きびきびした **genial** 愛想のいい 7 **fisherman** 釣り好きの人間 8 **inclined** ～しがちになった 9 **grumbled** 不平を言った 10 **vary** 変化をもたらす 12 **broad Scots** スコットランド訛り丸出しで
16 **inhabitant** 住人、患者 17 **inmates** 入院患者 **How he gets his information I haven't an idea** どうやって情報を得ているのか、まったくわからない 20 **old maid** オールドミス
25 **when you come to think of it** (you は一般人称) そのことを考えると 27 **sound lung between them** ふたりでひとつの健康な肺を共有している（ふたりともかなり病状がよくない） **loathe** 心から嫌っている

bell's room is just below McLeod's and Campbell plays the fiddle. It drives McLeod wild. He says he's been listening to the same tunes for fifteen years, but Campbell says McLeod doesn't know one tune from another. McLeod wants me to stop Campbell playing, but I can't do that, he's got a perfect right to play so long as he doesn't play in the silence hours. I've offered to change McLeod's room, but he won't do that. He says Campbell only plays to drive him out of the room because it's the best in the house, and he's damned if he's going to have it. It's queer, isn't it, that two middle-aged men should think it worth while to make life hell for one another? Neither can leave the other alone. They have their meals at the same table, they play bridge together; and not a day passes without a row. Sometimes I've threatened to turn them both out if they don't behave like sensible fellows. That keeps them quiet for a bit. They don't want to go. They've been here so long, they've got no one any more who gives a damn for them, and they can't cope with the world outside. Campbell went away for a couple of months' holiday some years ago. He came back after a week; he said he couldn't stand the racket, and the sight of so many people in the streets scared him.'

It was a strange world into which Ashenden found himself thrown when, his health gradually improving, he was able to mix with his fellow patients. One morning Dr Lennox told him he could thenceforward lunch in the dining-room. This was a large, low room,

2 **fiddle** バイオリン　**drives McLeod wild** マクラウドを怒らせる　3 **tunes** 曲　4 **doesn't know one tune from another**（another は another tune）曲の違いがわからない　6 **so long as** 〜であるかぎり　7 **silence hours** 静かにする時間　9 **drive...out** 追い出す　10 **damned** 呪われてしまう、死んだほうがましだ（be damned if 〜で、「断じて〜しない」）　**going to have it** そんなことをさせる　12 **worth while** 〜に値する　**make life hell for one another** たがいに相手を苦しめる　13 **leave the other alone** 他方を放っておく　15 **row** 騒ぎ　16 **turn...out** 放り出す　**sensible** 理性のある　19 **gives a damn** 気にかける　20 **cope with** 立ち向かう　22 **stand** 耐える　**the racket** 外の世界の騒々しさ

27 **fellow patients** 仲間の患者　28 **thenceforward** これからは

with great window space; the windows were always wide open and on fine days the sun streamed in. There seemed to be a great many people and it took him some time to sort them out. They were of all kinds, young, middle-aged, and old. There were some, like McLeod and Campbell, who had been at the sanatorium for years and expected to die there. Others had only been there for a few months. There was one middle-aged spinster called Miss Atkin who had been coming every winter for a long time and in the summer went to stay with friends and relations. She had nothing much the matter with her any more, and might just as well have stayed away altogether, but she liked the life. Her long residence had given her a sort of position, she was honorary librarian and hand in glove with the matron. She was always ready to gossip with you, but you were soon warned that everything you said was passed on. It was useful to Dr Lennox to know that his patients were getting on well together and were happy, that they did nothing imprudent and followed his instructions. Little escaped Miss Atkin's sharp eyes, and from her it went to the matron and so to Dr Lennox. Because she had been coming for so many years, she sat at the same table as McLeod and Campbell, together with an old general who had been put there on account of his rank. The table was in no way different from any other, and it was not more advantageously placed, but because the oldest residents sat there it was looked upon as the most desirable place to sit, and several elderly women

4 **sort...out** 種類分けする、見分ける 9 **spinster** 独身女性 11 **relations** 親戚 **had nothing much the matter with her any more** 彼女にはもうたいして悪いところはなかった 12 **might just as well have stayed away** ここにいなくてもかまわない 13 **altogether** まったく **the life** ここの生活 **long residence** ここで長く生活してきたこと 15 **honorary librarian** 名誉司書 **hand in glove** とても親しい **matron** 看護師長 16 **gossip with you**（you は一般人称）だれかれと噂話をする 17 **passed on** 伝わる 19 **getting on well together** みんな仲よくやっていく 20 **imprudent** 無分別な 21 **Little escaped Miss Atkin's sharp eyes** ミス・アトキンの鋭い耳を逃れるようなことはほとんどなかった **from her it went to the matron** 彼女から看護師長に伝わった 25 **general** 将軍 **rank** 地位 27 **advantageously** 都合良く 29 **desirable** 価値のある

were bitterly resentful because Miss Atkin, who went away for four or five months every summer, should be given a place there while they who spent the whole year in the sanatorium sat at other tables. There was an old Indian Civilian who had been at the sanatorium longer than anyone but McLeod and Campbell; he was a man who in his day had ruled a province, and he was waiting irascibly for either McLeod or Campbell to die so that he might take his place at the first table. Ashenden made the acquaintance of Campbell. He was a long, big-boned fellow with a bald head, so thin that you wondered how his limbs held together; and when he sat crumpled in an armchair he gave you the uncanny impression of a manikin in a puppetshow. He was brusque, touchy, and bad-tempered. The first thing he asked Ashenden was:

'Are you fond of music?'

'Yes.'

'No one here cares a damn for it. I play the violin. But if you like it, come to my room one day and I'll play to you.'

'Don't you go,' said McLeod, who heard him. 'It's torture.'

'How can you be so rude?' cried Miss Atkin. 'Mr Campbell plays very nicely.'

'There's no one in this beastly place that knows one note from another,' said Campbell.

With a derisive chuckle McLeod walked off. Miss Atkin tried to smooth things down.

'You mustn't mind what McLeod said.'

1 **resentful** 憤慨している 5 **Indian Civilian** インド行政官
6 **but** 以外 7 **had ruled a province**（英領インドの）ある州を治めていた 8 **irascibly** いらいらしながら 9 **the first table** いくつかあるテーブルのうち一番いいところにあるテーブル
10 **a long, big-boned fellow** 背の高い、骨太の男 11 **thin** 細い **how his limbs held together** どうやって全身の骨がくっついているのか 12 **sat crumpled** くしゃっと座った 13 **uncanny** 気味の悪い 14 **manikin in a puppetshow** 人形芝居の人形 **brusque** ぶっきらぼうな **touchy** 怒りっぽい 15 **bad-tempered** かんしゃく持ち
18 **No one here cares a damn for it**（it は音楽）ここの連中は音楽にはこれっぽっちも興味を持っていない
22 **torture** 拷問
25 **beastly** 野蛮な 26 **note** 曲
27 **a derisive chuckle** ばかにしたような笑い 28 **smooth things down** 場を治める、取りなす

'Oh, I don't. I'll get back on him all right.'

He played the same tune over and over again all that afternoon. McLeod banged on the floor, but Campbell went on. He sent a message by a maid to say that he had a headache and would Mr Campbell mind not playing; Campbell replied that he had a perfect right to play and if Mr McLeod didn't like it he could lump it. When next they met high words passed.

Ashenden was put at a table with the pretty Miss Bishop, with Templeton, and with a London man, an accountant, called Henry Chester. He was a stocky, broad-shouldered, wiry little fellow, and the last person you would ever have thought would be attacked by TB. It had come upon him as a sudden and unexpected blow. He was a perfectly ordinary man, somewhere between thirty and forty, married, with two children. He lived in a decent suburb. He went up to the City every morning and read the morning paper; he came down from the City every evening and read the evening paper. He had no interests except his business and his family. He liked his work; he made enough money to live in comfort, he put by a reasonable sum every year, he played golf on Saturday afternoon and on Sunday, he went every August for a three weeks' holiday to the same place on the east coast; his children would grow up and marry, then he would turn his business over to his son and retire with his wife to a little house in the country where he could potter about till death claimed him at a ripe old age. He asked nothing more from life than that, and it

1 **get back** 仕返しをする **all right** 絶対に
3 **banged** 蹴った 7 **lump**（不愉快なことを）我慢する
8 **high words** 厳しい言葉、激しい言葉
10 **accountant** 会計士 11 **stocky** ずんぐりした 12 **wiry** 体の引き締まった **the last person you would ever have thought would be attacked by TB**（you は一般人称）結核にかかると思われる最後の人間→とても結核にかかるとは思えない人間
14 **blow** 一撃、ショック 17 **decent** 住み心地のいい **the City** ロンドンのシティ（金融や商業の中心地） 22 **put by a reasonable sum** そこそこの貯金をしていた 26 **turn his business over** 仕事を引き継がせる 28 **potter** 散歩する **death claimed him** 死が彼をつかまえる **a ripe old age** 老年

was a life that thousands upon thousands of his fellow-men lived with satisfaction. He was the average citizen. Then this thing happened. He had caught cold playing golf, it had gone to his chest, and he had had a cough that he couldn't shake off. He had always been strong and healthy, and had no opinion of doctors; but at last at his wife's persuasion he had consented to see one. It was a shock to him, a fearful shock, to learn that there was tubercle in both his lungs and that his only chance of life was to go immediately to a sanatorium. The specialist he saw then told him that he might be able to go back to work in a couple of years, but two years had passed and Dr Lennox advised him not to think of it for at least a year more. He showed him the bacilli in his sputum, and in an X-ray photograph the actively-diseased patches in his lungs. He lost heart. It seemed to him a cruel and unjust trick that fate had played upon him. He could have understood it if he had led a wild life, if he had drunk too much, played around with women, or kept late hours. He would have deserved it then. But he had done none of these things. It was monstrously unfair. Having no resources in himself, no interest in books, he had nothing to do but think of his health. It became an obsession. He watched his symptoms anxiously. They had to deprive him of a thermometer because he took his temperature a dozen times a day. He got it into his head that the doctors were taking his case too indifferently, and in order to force their attention used every method he could devise to make the thermometer regis-

1 thousands upon thousands of his fellow-men 何千人もの（無数の）自分の仲間　5 shake off 振り払う、治す　6 had no opinion of doctors 医者というものをよく思っていなかった　7 persuasion 説得　9 tubercle 結核　14 bacilli (bacillus の複数形) バチルス菌　sputum 唾液　15 actively-diseased patches 進行性の結核の影　16 He lost heart 落胆した、失望した　17 unjust 不公平な　played upon 仕掛けた　18 wild life 放埒な生活　19 played around with women 女と遊び回る　kept late hours 夜更かしをする　20 He would have deserved it こんなことになってもしょうがない、自業自得だ　then (前の文の if 以下の仮定の部分を受けて) もしそうだったら　21 monstrously ひどく　22 resources 娯楽、趣味　24 obsession 強迫観念　symptoms 病状　anxiously 不安そうに　25 deprive 取りあげる　thermometer 体温計　26 got it into his head 思いこむ　27 case 症例、病気　28 in order to force their attention 彼ら (医者や看護師) の注意を引くために　used every method あらゆる手段を使った　29 devise 考案する　to make the thermometer register 体温計が示すようにする

ter a temperature that would alarm; and when his tricks were foiled he grew sulky and querulous. But he was by nature a jovial, friendly creature, and when he forgot himself he talked and laughed gaily; then on a sudden he remembered that he was a sick man and you would see in his eyes the fear of death.

At the end of every month his wife came up to spend a day or two in a lodging house near by. Dr Lennox did not much like the visits that relatives paid the patients, it excited and unsettled them. It was moving to see the eagerness with which Henry Chester looked forward to his wife's arrival; but it was strange to notice that once she had come he seemed less pleased than one would have expected. Mrs Chester was a pleasant, cheerful little woman, not pretty, but neat, as commonplace as her husband, and you only had to look at her to know that she was a good wife and mother, a careful housekeeper, a nice, quiet body who did her duty and interfered with nobody. She had been quite happy in the dull, domestic life they had led for so many years, her only dissipation a visit to the pictures, her great thrill the sales in the big London shops; and it had never occurred to her that it was monotonous. It completely satisfied her. Ashenden liked her. He listened with interest while she prattled about her children and her house in the suburbs, her neighbours and her trivial occupations. On one occasion he met her in the road. Chester for some reason connected with his treatment had stayed in and she was alone. Ashenden suggested that they should walk together.

1 alarm 危険を知らせる 2 foiled ばれる sulky 不機嫌な querulous 文句や不平をいう 3 by nature もともと jovial 陽気な creature 人間
8 lodging house 民宿 9 the visits that relatives paid the patients 親族や親戚が患者を見舞うこと 10 unsettled 落ち着きをなくす moving 心を動かす 11 eagerness 強い気持ち 13 less pleased than one would have expected (one は一般人称) 思ったほど喜ばなかった 15 neat こざっぱりした commonplace 平凡な 16 you only had to look at her to know 彼女をみさえすればわかる、一目でわかる 18 body 人 interfered 干渉した 20 dissipation 気晴らし、遊び 21 a visit to the pictures 映画館にいくこと 22 it had never occurred to her 彼女は思いもよらなかった 23 monotonous 退屈な、単調な 24 prattled あれこれ話した 26 trivial occupations ちょっとした趣味、時間つぶし 27 connected with his treatment 治療に関する

They talked for a little of indifferent things. Then she suddenly asked him how he thought her husband was.

'I think he seems to be getting on all right.'

'I'm so terribly worried.'

'You must remember it's a slow, long business. One has to have patience.'

They walked on a little and then he saw she was crying.

'You mustn't be unhappy about him,' said Ashenden gently.

'Oh, you don't know what I have to put up with when I come here. I know I ought not to speak about it, but I must. I can trust you, can't I?'

'Of course.'

'I love him. I'm devoted to him. I'd do anything in the world I could for him. We've never quarrelled, we've never even differed about a single thing. He's beginning to hate me and it breaks my heart.'

'Oh, I can't believe that. Why, when you're not here he talks of you all the time. He couldn't talk more nicely. He's devoted to you.'

'Yes, that's when I'm not here. It's when I'm here, when he sees me well and strong, that it comes over him. You see, he resents it so terribly that he's ill and I'm well. He's afraid he's going to die and he hates me because I'm going to live. I have to be on my guard all the time; almost everything I say, if I speak of the children, if I speak of the future, exasperates him, and he says bitter, wounding things. When I speak of some-

1 **indifferent things** どうでもいいこと、雑談
3 **getting on all right** 快復しつつある
5 **slow, long business** のろのろと時間のかかること
11 **put up with** 耐える、我慢する
15 **I'm devoted to him** 心から好きです　16 **in the world**（強調）
17 **differed** 意見が食い違った
19 **Why**（「なぜ」という意味の疑問詞ではなく、感嘆詞）いいですか　20 **couldn't talk more nicely** あれ以上ほめることはできないでしょう
22 **It's...that**（強調構文）　23 **strong** 体が丈夫　**it comes over him** 彼に変化が起こる　26 **on my guard** 防衛する、うっかりしたことをいわないように気をつける　28 **exasperates** 激怒させる　29 **wounding** 傷つけるような

thing I've had to do to the house or a servant I've had to change it irritates him beyond endurance. He complains that I treat him as if he didn't count any more. We used to be so united, and now I feel there's a great wall of antagonism between us. I know I shouldn't blame him, I know it's only his illness, he's a dear good man really, and kindness itself, normally he's the easiest man in the world to get on with; and now I simply dread coming here and I go with relief. He'd be terribly sorry if I had TB but I know that in his heart of hearts it would be a relief. He could forgive me, he could forgive fate, if he thought I was going to die too. Sometimes he tortures me by talking about what I shall do when he's dead, and when I get hysterical and cry out to him to stop, he says I needn't grudge him a little pleasure when he'll be dead so soon and I can go on living for years and years and have a good time. Oh, it's so frightful to think that this love we've had for one another all these years should die in this sordid, miserable way.'

Mrs Chester sat down on a stone by the roadside and gave way to passionate weeping. Ashenden looked at her with pity, but could find nothing to say that might comfort her. What she had told him did not come quite as a surprise.

'Give me a cigarette,' she said at last. 'I mustn't let my eyes get all red and swollen, or Henry'll know I've been crying and he'll think I've had bad news about him. Is death so horrible? Do we all fear death like that?'

2 **beyond endurance** 忍耐の限界を超える　3 **didn't count any more** もうどうでもいい　5 **antagonism** 反目、反感　8 **get on with** うまくやっていく　**dread** 恐れる　12 **tortures** いやな思いをさせる、苦しませる　15 **grudge him a little pleasure** 彼のささやかな喜びに不平をいう　19 **sordid** みすぼらしい、暗い　21 **gave way to passionate weeping** 激しく泣きだした　26 **swollen** 腫れた状態

'I don't know,' said Ashenden.

'When my mother was dying she didn't seem to mind a bit. She knew it was coming and she even made little jokes about it. But she was an old woman.'

Mrs Chester pulled herself together and they set off again. They walked for a while in silence.

'You won't think any the worse of Henry for what I've told you?' she said at last.

'Of course not.'

'He's been a good husband and a good father. I've never known a better man in my life. Until this illness I don't think an unkind or ungenerous thought ever passed through his head.'

The conversation left Ashenden pensive. People often said he had a low opinion of human nature. It was because he did not always judge his fellows by the usual standards. He accepted, with a smile, a tear, or a shrug of the shoulders, much that filled others with dismay. It was true that you would never have expected that good-natured, commonplace little chap to harbour such bitter and unworthy thoughts; but who has ever been able to tell to what depths man may fall or to what heights rise? The fault lay in the poverty of his ideals. Henry Chester was born and bred to lead an average life, exposed to the normal vicissitudes of existence, and when an unforeseeable accident befell him he had no means of coping with it. He was like a brick made to take its place with a million others in a huge factory, but by chance with a flaw in it so that it is inadequate to its

5 **pulled herself together** 気を取り直した　**set off** 歩きだした
7 **think any the worse of Henry** ヘンリーのことを悪く思う
12 **ungenerous** 心の狭い
14 **pensive** 考えこんだ状態　15 **low opinion** 低く考えること
18 **filled others with dismay** ほかの人の心を落胆や失望でいっぱいにする　20 **commonplace** どこにでもいるような　**chap** 男　**harbour** 心に抱く　**bitter and unworthy thoughts** 恨みがましい、下らない考え　22 **tell** 知る　23 **fault** 過ち（の原因）　**the poverty of his ideals** 理想の貧困さ　24 **bred** 育った　**exposed** さらされた　25 **vicissitudes of existence** 人生の変化　26 **unforeseeable** 予想もしなかった　**befell** 降りかかった　**means** 手段　29 **flaw** きず、不備　**inadequate** 不適当、使い物にならない

purpose. And the brick too, if it had a mind, might cry: What have I done that I cannot fulfil my modest end, but must be taken away from all these other bricks that support me and thrown on the dust-heap? It was no fault of Henry Chester's that he was incapable of the conceptions that might have enabled him to bear his calamity with resignation. It is not everyone who can find solace in art or thought. It is the tragedy of our day that these humble souls have lost their faith in God, in whom lay hope, and their belief in a resurrection that might bring them the happiness that has been denied them on earth; and have found nothing to put in their place.

There are people who say that suffering ennobles. It is not true. As a general rule it makes man petty, querulous, and selfish; but here in this sanatorium there was not much suffering. In certain stages of tuberculosis the slight fever that accompanies it excites rather than depresses, so that the patient feels alert and, upborne by hope, faces the future blithely; but for all that the idea of death haunts the subconscious. It is a sardonic theme song that runs through a sprightly operetta. Now and again the gay, melodious arias, the dance measures, deviate strangely into tragic strains that throb menacingly down the nerves; the petty interests of every day, the small jealousies and trivial concerns are as nothing; pity and terror make the heart on a sudden stand still and the awfulness of death broods as the silence that precedes a tropical storm broods over the tropical jungle. After Ashenden had been for some time at the sanatorium

2 **What have I done** いったい自分がどんな（悪い、まずい）ことをしたというのだ **fulfil my modest end** ささやかな目的を果たす 4 **dust-heap** ゴミの山 5 **incapable of the conceptions** that 以下のような考えを持つことができない 6 **bear** 耐える **calamity** 災厄 7 **resignation** あきらめ **solace** なぐさめ 9 **humble** つましい、普通の 10 **resurrection** 復活 **bring them the happiness** 彼らに幸せをもたらす 11 **them**（2つあるが両方とも）つましい、普通の人々

13 **ennobles** 気高くする 14 **petty** 狭量 **querulous** 不平ばかりいう 16 **stages** 段階 18 **depresses** 落ちこませる **alert** 敏活な **upborne** 高揚感を持つ 19 **blithely** 楽しげに、陽気に **for all that** それでも 20 **haunts** とりついて離れない **sardonic** 冷笑的な **theme song** テーマソング 21 **sprightly operetta** 陽気なオペレッタ **Now and again** ときどき 22 **arias** アリア **dance measures** 踊りの音楽、調子 **deviate** それる 23 **strains** 調子 **throb** 大きく動悸をうつ **menacingly** おびやかすように 24 **petty interests** どうでもいい興味 25 **trivial concerns** ささいな不安 **as nothing** 取るに足らない 26 **sudden stand still** 突然の休止 27 **broods** おおう **precedes** 〜に先立つ、〜の前触れの 28 **tropical storm** 熱帯の嵐

there came a boy of twenty. He was in the navy, a sub-lieutenant in a submarine, and he had what they used to call in novels galloping consumption. He was a tall, good-looking youth, with curly brown hair, blue eyes, and a very sweet smile. Ashenden saw him two or three times lying on the terrace in the sun and passed the time of day with him. He was a cheerful lad. He talked of musical shows and film stars; and he read the paper for the football results and the boxing news. Then he was put to bed and Ashenden saw him no more. His relations were sent for and in two months he was dead. He died uncomplaining. He understood what was happening to him as little as an animal. For a day or two there was the same malaise in the sanatorium as there is in a prison when a man has been hanged; and then, as though by universal consent, in obedience to an instinct of self-preservation, the boy was put out of mind: life, with its three meals a day, its golf on the miniature course, its regulated exercise, its prescribed rests, its quarrels and jealousies, its scandalmongering and petty vexations, went on as before. Campbell, to the exasperation of McLeod, continued to play the prize-song and 'Annie Laurie' on his fiddle. McLeod continued to boast of his bridge and gossip about other people's health and morals. Miss Atkin continued to backbite. Henry Chester continued to complain that the doctors gave him insufficient attention and railed against fate because, after the model life he had led, it had played him such a dirty trick. Ashenden continued to read, and with amused tol-

Sanatorium

1 sub-lieutenant 海軍中尉 2 submarine 潜水艦 3 call in novels galloping consumption 小説ではよく「奔馬性肺結核」と書かれる 6 the time of day 昼間のひととき 7 lad 青年 9 football サッカー 10 relations 親戚 11 were sent for 呼ばれた in two months 2カ月後 14 malaise 不安、暗さ 15 hanged 処刑される by universal consent 全体の合意、全員の合意 16 self-preservation 自己保存 17 was put out of mind 忘れられた 19 prescribed 決められた 20 scandalmongering 人の悪口 petty vexations つまらないいらだち 21 exasperation 激怒 22 prize-song 優勝の歌、朝はバラ色に輝きて（ワーグナー「ニュルンベルクのマイスタージンガー」3幕5場） 25 backbite 陰口をきく 27 railed ののしった 28 the model life 模範的な人生 dirty trick 汚い手口 29 amused tolerance 大らかな気持ちで楽しんでいた

erance to watch the vagaries of his fellowcreatures.

He became intimate with Major Templeton. Templeton was perhaps a little more than forty years of age. He had been in the Grenadier Guards, but had resigned his commission after the war. A man of ample means, he had since then devoted himself entirely to pleasure. He raced in the racing season, shot in the shooting season, and hunted in the hunting season. When this was over he went to Monte Carlo. He told Ashenden of the large sums he had made and lost at baccarat. He was very fond of women and if his stories could be believed they were very fond of him. He loved good food and good drink. He knew by their first names the head waiters of every restaurant in London where you ate well. He belonged to half a dozen clubs. He had led for years a useless, selfish, worthless life, the sort of life which maybe it will be impossible for anyone to live in the future, but he had lived it without misgiving and had enjoyed it. Ashenden asked him once what he would do if he had his time over again and he answered that he would do exactly what he had done. He was an amusing talker, gay and pleasantly ironic, and he dealt with the surface of things, which was all he knew, with a light, easy, and assured touch. He always had a pleasant word for the dowdy spinsters in the sanatorium and a joking one for the peppery old gentlemen, for he combined good manners with a natural kindliness. He knew his way about the superficial world of the people who have more money than they know what to do with as well

1 **vagaries** とっぴな行為　**fellowcreatures** 仲間
4 **Grenadier Guards** 近衛歩兵連隊　5 **commission** 軍務　**ample** 豊かな　**means** 財産、資産　7 **raced** 馬に乗った　**shooting season** 狩猟のシーズン　9 **Monte Carlo** モンテカルロ（モナコ北東部の観光地で、カジノで有名）　**the large sums** 多額　10 **baccarat** バカラ（カジノで行われるトランプを使ったギャンブル）　14 **ate well** おいしく食事のできる　18 **misgiving** 不安、気づかい　20 **had his time over again** 人生をやり直す　21 **amusing talker** 話のうまい人　22 **dealt with the surface of things** 物事の表面を扱った　23 **with a light, easy, and assured touch** 軽く、気軽に、自信たっぷりに　25 **dowdy** みすぼらしい　**spinsters** 独身女性　26 **peppery** 短気な　27 **knew his way** 自分なりのやり方がわかっていた（He knew his way about the superficial world...as well as he knew his way about Mayfair）28 **superficial** 表面的な、浅い　**people who have more money than they know what to do with** どう使っていいかわからないくらい金を持っている連中　29 **as well as** 〜と同様に

as he knew his way about Mayfair. He was the kind of man who would always have been willing to take a bet, to help a friend, and to give a tenner to a rogue. If he had never done much good in the world he had never done much harm. He amounted to nothing. But he was a more agreeable companion than many of more sterling character and of more admirable qualities. He was very ill now. He was dying and he knew it. He took it with the same easy, laughing nonchalance as he had taken all the rest. He'd had a thundering good time, he regretted nothing, it was rotten tough luck getting TB but to hell with it, no one can live for ever, and when you came to think of it, he might have been killed in the war or broken his bloody neck in a point-to-point. His principle all through life had been, when you've made a bad bet, pay up and forget about it. He'd had a good run for his money and he was ready to call it a day. It had been a damned good party while it lasted, but every party's got to come to an end, and next day it doesn't matter much if you went home with the milk or if you left while the fun was in full swing.

Of all those people in the sanatorium he was probably from the moral standpoint the least worthy, but he was the only one who genuinely accepted the inevitable with unconcern. He snapped his fingers in the face of death, and you could choose whether to call his levity unbecoming or his insouciance gallant.

The last thing that ever occurred to him when he came to the sanatorium was that he might fall more deeply in

1 he knew his way about Mayfair メイフェア（当時はロンドンの中心にある高級住宅地で、社交界の有名人たちが住んでいた）の地理に明るかった   2 take a bet 賭をする   3 tenner 10 ポンド   rogue 浮浪者   5 amounted to nothing 価値がなかった、どうでもいい人間だった   6 sterling 立派な   9 nonchalance 無頓着さ   10 the rest ほかのこと   thundering good time とんでもなく楽しい時   11 rotten tough luck getting TB 結核になるというまったくの悪運   to hell with it そんなことを気にしてたまるか   12 when you came to think of it (youは一般人称)考えてみれば   14 broken his bloody neck 首の骨を折っていた   point-to-point クロスカントリー競馬   16 pay up 支払う   He'd had a good run for his money 彼にとっては満足感があった、楽しかった   17 call it a day 終わりにする   It had been a damned good party 思いきり楽しいパーティだった   18 while it lasted 続いていた間は   20 went home with the milk 朝帰りをする   while the fun was in full swing とてもにぎやかなあいだに

23 moral standpoint 道徳的な観点からみて   24 the inevitable 避けられないこと、死   with unconcern 無関心に   25 snapped his fingers in the face of death 死神の顔の前で指を鳴らした   26 levity 軽さ   unbecoming 不適切   27 insouciance 無頓着さ   gallant 立派な

love there than he had ever done before. His amours had been numerous, but they had been light; he had been content with the politely mercenary love of chorus girls and with ephemeral unions with women of easy virtue whom he met at house parties. He had always taken care to avoid any attachment that might endanger his freedom. His only aim in life had been to get as much fun out of it as possible, and where sex was concerned he found every advantage and no inconvenience in ceaseless variety. But he liked women. Even when they were quite old he could not talk to them without a caress in his eyes and a tenderness in his voice. He was prepared to do anything to please them. They were conscious of his interest in them and were agreeably flattered, and they felt, quite mistakenly, that they could trust him never to let them down. He once said a thing that Ashenden thought showed insight:

'You know, any man can get any woman he wants if he tries hard enough, there's nothing in that, but once he's got her, only a man who thinks the world of women can get rid of her without humiliating her.'

It was simply from habit that he began to make love to Ivy Bishop. She was the prettiest and the youngest girl in the sanatorium. She was in point of fact not so young as Ashenden had first thought her, she was twenty-nine, but for the last eight years she had been wandering from one sanatorium to another, in Switzerland, England, and Scotland, and the sheltered invalid life had preserved her youthful appearance so that you

1 **amours** 色恋　2 **light** 軽い　3 **mercenary** 金目当て　**chorus girls** コーラスガール（ショーやレビューなどのバックで歌ったり踊ったりする女性）　4 **ephemeral unions** つかの間の交際　**women of easy virtue** だらしのない女　6 **attachment** 愛情、恋愛　9 **advantage** 利点　**inconvenience** 不便　**ceaseless variety** たえず相手が変わること　11 **caress** 優しさ　14 **agreeably** 快く　**flattered** うれしくなった　16 **let them down** 捨てる　**that Ashenden thought showed insight**（Ashenden thoughtは挿入句）洞察力を表しているとアシェンデンが思った
19 **there's nothing in that** そんなことはたいしたことじゃない
21 **get rid of her without humiliating her** 相手を傷つけることなく捨てる
22 **It was...that**（強調構文）　**make love to** 言いよる　24 **in point of fact** 実際には　28 **sheltered**（外から）防御された　**invalid** 病気の

might easily have taken her for twenty. All she knew of the world she had learnt in these establishments, so that she combined rather curiously extreme innocence with extreme sophistication. She had seen a number of love affairs run their course. A good many men, of various nationalities, had made love to her; she accepted their attentions with self-possession and humour, but she had at her disposal plenty of firmness when they showed an inclination to go too far. She had a force of character unexpected in anyone who looked so flower-like, and when it came to a show-down knew how to express her meaning in plain, cool, and decisive words. She was quite ready to have a flirtation with George Templeton. It was a game she understood, and though always charming to him, it was with a bantering lightness that showed quite clearly that she had summed him up and had no mind to take the affair more seriously than he did. Like Ashenden, Templeton went to bed every evening at six and dined in his room, so that he saw Ivy only by day. They went for little walks together, but otherwise were seldom alone. At lunch the conversation between the four of them, Ivy, Templeton, Henry Chester, and Ashenden, was general, but it was obvious that it was for neither of the two men that Templeton took so much trouble to be entertaining. It seemed to Ashenden that he was ceasing to flirt with Ivy to pass the time, and that his feeling for her was growing deeper and more sincere; but he could not tell whether she was conscious of it nor whether it meant anything to her. Whenever

2 **these establishments** こういった施設（病院） 3 **innocence** 無邪気さ 4 **sophistication** 世慣れていること、様子 **love affairs** 恋愛 5 **run their course** それなりの道をたどる 7 **self-possession** 冷静さ 8 **at her disposal** 自分の好きなように **plenty of firmness** 断固とした態度、言葉 9 **force of character** 性格の強さ 10 **flower-like** 花のような 11 **show-down** 決着をつけるとき **express her meaning** 自分の思っていることをいう 13 **have a flirtation** 軽い恋愛を楽しむ 15 **charming to him** 彼を喜ばせる **with a bantering lightness** からかい半分の軽さでもって 16 **summed him up** 彼のことは大体わかっている 17 **the affair** このこと、軽い気持ちで付き合ってること 20 **only by day** 昼間だけ 21 **alone** ふたりきり 25 **much trouble to be entertaining** わざわざ楽しませる

Templeton hazarded a remark that was more intimate than the occasion warranted she countered it with an ironic one that made them all laugh. But Templeton's laugh was rueful. He was no longer content to have her take him as a play-boy. The more Ashenden knew Ivy Bishop the more he liked her. There was something pathetic in her sick beauty, with that lovely transparent skin, the thin face in which the eyes were so large and so wonderfully blue; and there was something pathetic in her plight, for like so many others in the sanatorium she seemed to be alone in the world. Her mother led a busy social life, her sisters were married; they took but a perfunctory interest in the young woman from whom they had been separated now for eight years. They corresponded, they came to see her occasionally, but there was no longer very much between them. She accepted the situation without bitterness. She was friendly with everyone and prepared always to listen with sympathy to the complaints and the distress of all and sundry. She went out of her way to be nice to Henry Chester and did what she could to cheer him.

'Well, Mr Chester,' she said to him one day at lunch, 'it's the end of the month, your wife will be coming tomorrow. That's something to look forward to.'

'No, she's not coming this month,' he said quietly, looking down at his plate.

'Oh, I am sorry. Why not? The children are all right, aren't they?'

'Dr Lennox thinks it's better for me that she shouldn't

1 **hazarded** 思い切っていった **remark** 言葉 2 **occasion warranted** その場が許す **countered** 反撃した 4 **rueful** 悲しげ 7 **pathetic** 悲愴な 10 **plight** 苦境 12 **but**（=only） 13 **a perfunctory interest** おざなりの興味 17 **without bitterness** 文句をいわずに 19 **all and sundry** 全員 20 **out of her way** わざわざ〜する

come.'

There was a silence. Ivy looked at him with troubled eyes.

'That's tough luck, old man,' said Templeton in his hearty way. 'Why didn't you tell Lennox to go to hell?'

'He must know best,' said Chester.

Ivy gave him another look and began to talk of something else.

Looking back, Ashenden realized that she had at once suspected the truth. For next day he happened to walk with Chester.

'I'm awfully sorry your wife isn't coming,' he said. 'You'll miss her visit dreadfully.'

'Dreadfully.'

He gave Ashenden a sidelong glance. Ashenden felt that he had something he wanted to say, but could not bring himself to say it. He gave his shoulders an angry shrug.

'It's my fault if she's not coming. I asked Lennox to write and tell her not to. I couldn't stick it any more. I spend the whole month looking forward to her coming and then when she's here I hate her. You see, I resent so awfully having this filthy disease. She's strong and well and full of beans. It maddens me when I see the pain in her eyes. What does it matter to her really? Who cares if you're ill? They pretend to care, but they're jolly glad it's you and not them. I'm a swine, aren't I?'

Ashenden remembered how Mrs Chester had sat on a stone by the side of the road and wept.

4 **tough luck** 不幸、辛いこと　5 **go to hell** くたばれ
13 **miss** 残念に思う　**dreadfully** とても
15 **a sidelong glance** 横目でちらりとみること　16 **could not bring himself to say it** それをいう気にはなれなかった
20 **stick it** 我慢する　23 **filthy** いやらしい　24 **full of beans** 元気ではつらつとしている　**maddens** いらつかせる、しゃくに障る　26 **jolly** とても　27 **it's you and not them** 病気になったのが相手であって自分ではない　**swine** 豚、いやなやつ

'Aren't you afraid you'll make her very unhappy, not letting her come?'

'She must put up with that. I've got enough with my own unhappiness without bothering with hers.'

Ashenden did not know what to say and they walked on in silence. Suddenly Chester broke out irritably.

'It's all very well for you to be disinterested and unselfish, you're going to live. I've going to die, and God damn it, I don't want to die. Why should I? It's not fair.'

Time passed. In a place like the sanatorium where there was little to occupy the mind it was inevitable that soon everyone should know that George Templeton was in love with Ivy Bishop. But it was not so easy to tell what her feelings were. It was plain that she liked his company, but she did not seek it, and indeed it looked as though she took pains not to be alone with him. One or two of the middle-aged ladies tried to trap her into some compromising admission, but ingenuous as she was, she was easily a match for them. She ignored their hints and met their straight questions with incredulous laughter. She succeeded in exasperating them.

'She can't be so stupid as not to see that he's mad about her.'

'She has no right to play with him like that.'

'I believe she's just as much in love with him as he is with her.'

'Dr Lennox ought to tell her mother.'

No one was more incensed than McLeod.

'Too ridiculous. After all, nothing can come of it.

1 **not letting her come** 彼女をこさせないことで
3 **put up** 我慢する **got enough with** 〜で十分だ、〜だけで十分しんどい 4 **bothering with hers** 彼女にかまってやること
7 **disinterested and unselfish** 無関心で寛大 8 **God damn it** くそっ
11 **little to occupy the mind** 考えることがほとんどない **it was inevitable**（it は that 以下）避けられなかった 16 **she took pains not to be alone with him** なるべく彼とふたりきりにならないようにした 18 **compromising admission** しかたなく認めること **ingenuous as she was** 彼女は無邪気だったが 19 **a match** 対等の相手、ひけをとらない **hints** ほのめかし 20 **met** 答えた **straight questions** あけすけな質問 **incredulous** まさかといわんばかりの 21 **exasperating** いらいらさせる
24 **play with** もてあそぶ
28 **was...incensed** 怒った
29 **nothing can come of it** なんにもならない

He's riddled with TB and she's not much better.'

Campbell on the other hand was sardonic and gross.

'I'm all for their having a good time while they can. I bet there's a bit of hanky-panky going on if one only knew, and I don't blame 'em.'

'You cad,' said McLeod.

'Oh, come off it. Templeton isn't the sort of chap to play bumble-puppy bridge with a girl like that unless he's getting something out of it, and she knows a thing or two, I bet.'

Ashenden, who saw most of them, knew them better than any of the others. Templeton at last had taken him into his confidence. He was rather amused at himself.

'Rum thing at my time of life, falling in love with a decent girl. Last thing I'd ever expected of myself. And it's no good denying it, I'm in it up to the neck; if I were a well man I'd ask her to marry me tomorrow. I never knew a girl could be as nice as that. I've always thought girls, decent girl, I mean, damned bores. But she isn't a bore, she's as clever as she can stick. And pretty too. My God, what a skin! And that hair: but it isn't any of that that's bowled me over like a row of ninepins. D'you know what's got me? Damned ridiculous when you come to think of it. An old rip like me. Virtue. Makes me laugh like a hyena. Last thing I've ever wanted in a woman, but there it is, no getting away from it, she's good, and it makes me feel like a worm. Surprises you, I suppose?'

'Not a bit,' said Ashenden. 'You're not the first rake

1 **He's riddled with TB** 彼は結核にやられている
2 **sardonic** 冷笑的　**gross** いやらしい
3 **all for** 賛成する、大いに認める　4 **hanky-panky going on** 恋愛ごっこが進行中　**if one only knew**（one は一般人称）だれもが当然知っているだろうが
6 **cad** 人非人、人でなし
7 **come off it** やめてくれ　8 **play bumble-puppy bridge with a girl like that** あのような女の子にちょっかいを出す　9 **getting something out of it** 何か目的がある、下心がある　**knows a thing or two** 多少のことは知っている
12 **taken him into his confidence** アシェンデンに打ち明けた
13 **He was rather amused at himself** テンプルトンは自分のことをおもしろがっていた
14 **Rum** 不思議な　16 **up to the neck** 完全に　17 **well man** 元気な人間　19 **damned bores** むちゃくちゃ退屈　20 **as clever as she can stick** とても頭がいい　22 **bowled me over** 打ちのめした、はじき飛ばした　**row of ninepins** 9本のピン（9本のピンを使ったボウリングにたとえている）　23 **what's got me** わたしの心をつかんだもの　24 **rip** 遊び人　**Makes me laugh like a hyena** （そのことは）わたしをハイエナのように笑わせる
25 **Last thing I've ever wanted in a woman** わたしが女に求めていた最後のもの→わたしが女にまったく求めなかったもの
26 **no getting away from it** それから逃げられない　27 **worm** ウジ虫
29 **rake** 遊び人

who's fallen to innocence. It's merely the sentimentality of middle age.'

'Dirty dog,' laughed Templeton.

'What does she say to it?'

'Good God, you don't suppose I've told her. I've never said a word to her that I wouldn't have said before anyone else. I may be dead in six months, and besides, what have I got to offer a girl like that?'

Ashenden by now was pretty sure that she was just as much in love with Templeton as he was with her. He had seen the flush that coloured her cheeks when Templeton came into the dining-room and he had noticed the soft glance she gave him now and then when he was not looking at her. There was a peculiar sweetness in her smile when she listened to him telling some of his old experiences. Ashenden had the impression that she basked comfortably in his love as the patients on the terrace, facing the snow, basked in the hot sunshine; but it might very well be that she was content to leave it at that, and it was certainly no business of his to tell Templeton what perhaps she had no wish that he should know.

Then an incident occurred to disturb the monotony of life. Though McLeod and Campbell was always at odds they played bridge together because, till Templeton came, they were the best players in the sanatorium. They bickered incessantly, their post-mortems were endless, but after so many years each knew the other's game perfectly and they took a keen delight in scoring

1 **innocence** 無邪気な人
3 **Dirty dog** いやなやつ
5 **Good God** これは驚いた 7 **in six months** 6カ月後
8 **what have I got to offer a girl like that?** わたしに、あんな女の子に差しだすものがありますか？
11 **flush** 赤味 13 **now and then** ときどき 14 **peculiar** 独特の
17 **basked** ひなたぼっこをしている 19 **it might very well be that** that 以下のことはあり得る **leave it at that** いまのままの状態にしておく
24 **at odds** 敵対して、いがみあって 27 **bickered** 口げんかをしていた **incessantly** ひっきりなしに **post-mortems** 死体解剖→ゲームが終わったあとの検討や分析 29 **scoring off** やりこめる、出し抜く

off one another. As a rule Templeton refused to play with them; though a fine player he preferred to play with Ivy Bishop, and McLeod and Campbell were agreed on this, that she ruined the game. She was the kind of player who, having made a mistake that lost the rubber, would laugh and say: Well, it only made the difference of a trick. But one afternoon, since Ivy was staying in her room with a headache, Templeton consented to play with Campbell and McLeod. Ashenden was the fourth. Though it was the end of March there had been heavy snow for several days, and they played, in a veranda open on three sides to the wintry air, in fur coats and caps, with mittens on their hands. The stakes were too small for a gambler like Templeton to take the game seriously and his bidding was overbold, but he played so much better than the other three that he generally managed to make his contract or at least to come near it. But there was much doubling and redoubling. The cards ran high, so that an inordinate number of small slams were bid; it was a tempestuous game, and McLeod and Campbell lashed one another with their tongues. Half past five arrived and the last rubber was started, for at six the bell rang to send everyone to rest. It was a hard-fought rubber, with sets on both sides, for McLeod and Campbell were opponents and each was determined that the other should not win. At ten minutes to six it was game all and the last hand was dealt. Templeton was McLeod's partner and Ashenden Campbell's. The bidding started with two clubs from McLeod; Ashenden

1 **As a rule** いつもは　5 **rubber** 勝負　7 **a trick** トリック（コントラクトブリッジでは、7～13回のトリックで1回の勝負が決まる）　**since** ～だったので　12 **wintry air** 冬の空気　13 **mittens** ミトン　15 **bidding** ビッド（ディクレアラーになるという意思表示）　**overbold** 大胆すぎる　17 **make his contract** ビッド（ブリッジで何トリックで勝つかを宣言）してそれを達成すること　**come near it** それに近いところまでいく　18 **doubling** ダブル（相手の提示したコントラクトを達成できないと思った場合に使う）　**redoubling** リダブル（相手にダブルをかけられたとき、それでもコントラクトを達成する自信があるときに使う）　19 **ran high** ハイレベルになった　**inordinate** 異常な　**small slams** リトルスラム（13回のトリックのうち12回取ること）　20 **were bid** 宣言された　**tempestuous** 大荒れの　21 **lashed** 攻撃した　**with their tongues** 言葉で　23 **send everyone to rest** 全員を部屋に戻って寝させる　**a hardfought rubber** 激しい戦い　24 **with sets on both sides** 勝負の流れが両方に向いている　26 **the other should not win**（should は話者の意志を表す助動詞）相手には勝たせない　27 **game all** 最終戦　29 **two clubs** クラブの2

※ビッド「何トリック以上獲得することを勝つ条件にして、どのカードをトランプ（切り札）にするか」を順番に宣言すること。もっとも多く獲得すると宣言したプレイヤーが「ディクレアラー」になる。

said nothing; Templeton showed that he had substantial help, and finally McLeod called a grand slam. Campbell doubled and McLeod redoubled. Hearing this, the players at other tables who had broken off gathered round and the hands were played in deadly silence to a little crowd of onlookers. McLeod's face was white with excitement and there were beads of sweat on his brow. His hands trembled. Campbell was very grim. McLeod had to take two finesses and they both came off. He finished with a squeeze and got the last of the thirteen tricks. There was a burst of applause from the onlookers. McLeod, arrogant in victory, sprang to his feet. He shook his clenched fist at Campbell.

'Play that off on your blasted fiddle,' he shouted. 'Grand slam doubled and redoubled. I've wanted to get it all my life and now I've got it. By God, By God.'

He gasped. He staggered forward and fell across the table. A stream of blood poured from his mouth. The doctor was sent for. Attendants came. He was dead.

He was buried two days later, early in the morning so that the patients should not be disturbed by the sight of a funeral. A relation in black came from Glasgow to attend it. No one had liked him. No one regretted him. At the end of a week so far as one could tell, he was forgotten. The Indian Civilian took his place at the principal table and Campbell moved into the room he had so long wanted.

'Now we shall have peace,' said Dr Lennox to Ashenden. 'When you think that I've had to put up with the

1 **substantial** しっかりした 2 **grand slam** グランドスラム（13回のトリックすべてに勝つこと） 4 **broken off** ゲームを中止した 5 **to a little crowd** 少人数の集まり 6 **onlookers** 見物人 7 **brow** 額 8 **grim** しかめっ面 9 **finesses** フィネス（強い手札を残して、弱い手札でトリックを取ること） **came off** 成功した 10 **squeeze** スクイズ（相手に強い札を捨てさせること） 11 **applause** 拍手喝采 12 **sprang to his feet** ぱっと立ち上がった 13 **clenched fist** 握り拳

14 **Play that off** こういうことをやってみろ **on your blasted fiddle** おまえのぼろバイオリンで 16 **By God** やった 17 **gasped** あえいだ **staggered forward** ぐらっと前に傾いた **across the table** テーブルの上に 19 **Attendants** 介護人

21 **be disturbed** 不安になる 22 **A relation in black** 喪服を着た親戚 **Glasgow** グラスゴー（スコットランド中南部の港町） 24 **so far as one could tell**（one は一般人称）みんなの知る限りでは 25 **the principal table**（P104、P105 の the first table と同じ）一番いい場所にあるテーブル

quarrels and complaints of those two men for years and years . . . Believe me, one has to have patience to run a sanatorium. And to think that after all the trouble he's given me he had to end up like that and scare all those people out of their wits.'

'It was a bit of a shock, you know,' said Ashenden.

'He was a worthless fellow and yet some of the women have been quite upset about it. Poor little Miss Bishop cried her eyes out.'

'I suspect that she was the only one who cried for him and not for herself.'

But presently it appeared that there was one person who had not forgotten him. Campbell went about like a lost dog. He wouldn't play bridge. He wouldn't talk. There was no doubt about it, he was moping for McLeod. For several days he remained in his room, having his meals brought to him, and then went to Dr Lennox and said he didn't like it as well as his old one and wanted to be moved back. Dr Lennox lost his temper, which he rarely did, and told him he had been pestering him to give him that room for years and now he could stay there or get out of the sanatorium. He returned to it and sat gloomily brooding.

'Why don't you play your violin?' the matron asked him at length. 'I haven't heard you play for a fortnight.'

'I haven't.'

'Why not?'

'It's no fun any more. I used to get a kick out of playing because I knew it maddened McLeod. But now no-

2 **patience** 忍耐　**run** 経営する、やっていく　3 **to think that**（that 以下のことを受けて）まったく、どういっていいのか　**after all the trouble he's given me** わたしにあれだけ苦労をかけたあとで　4 **he had to end up like that** あんなふうに死んでいった　**scare all those people out of their wits** みんなをぞっとさせた

7 **and yet** しかし　9 **cried her eyes out** 目玉がこぼれるほど泣いた

10 **cried for him and not for herself** 自分のためでなく彼のために泣いた

13 **went about** 歩きまわった　14 **lost dog** 迷い犬　15 **moping** ふさぎこんでいる　19 **be moved back**（元の部屋に）もどる　**lost his temper** 怒った　20 **pestering** 困らせる　23 **gloomily** 鬱々と　**brooding** くよくよする

24 **matron** 看護師長　25 **at length** そのうち　**fortnight** 2週間
28 **get a kick** 快感を覚える

body cares if I play or not. I shall never play again.'

Nor did he for all the rest of the time that Ashenden was at the sanatorium. It was strange, now that McLeod was dead, life had lost its savour for him. With no one to quarrel with, no one to infuriate, he had lost his incentive and it was plain that it would not be long before he followed his enemy to the grave.

But on Templeton McLeod's death had another effect, and one which was soon to have unexpected consequences. He talked to Ashenden about it in his cool, detached way.

'Grand, passing out like that in his moment of triumph. I can't make out why everyone got in such a state about it. He'd been here for years, hadn't he?'

'Eighteen, I believe.'

'I wonder if it's worth it. I wonder if it's not better to have one's fling and take the consequences.'

'I suppose it depends on how much you value life.'

'But is this life?'

Ashenden had no answer. In a few months he could count on being well, but you only had to look at Templeton to know that he was not going to recover. The death-look was on his face.

'D'you know what I've done?' asked Templeton. 'I've asked Ivy to marry me.'

Ashenden was startled.

'What did she say?'

'Bless her little heart, she said it was the most ridiculous idea she'd ever heard in her life and I was crazy to

2 **rest of the time that Ashenden was at the sanatorium** アシェンデンがサナトリウムにいる間ずっと 4 **savour** 味 5 **infuriate** 怒らせる **incentive** 刺激、励み

11 **detached** 超然とした、冷静な

12 **Grand** 素晴らしい **passing out** 死ぬこと 13 **make out** 理解する **everyone got in such a state** みんながあんな状態でいる 14 **about it** マクラウドが死んだことで

16 **it's** (it は Eighteen) **worth it** それだけの価値がある **if it's not better to** to 以下をしたほうがよくないのか 17 **have one's fling** やりたいようにやる **take the consequences** その結果を引き受ける

18 **how much you value life** 生きているということをどのくらい重要だと思うか

19 **is this life?** これが生きているといえますか?

21 **count on being well** 快復することを期待する 22 **he** (=Templeton)

26 **was startled** 驚いた

28 **Bless her little heart** 彼女のかわいい心に祝福がありますように

think of such a thing.'

'You must admit she was right.'

'Quite. But she's going to marry me.'

'It's madness.'

'I dare say it is; but anyhow, we're going to see Lennox and ask him what he thinks about it.'

The winter had broken at last; there was still snow on the hills, but in the valleys it was melted and on the lower slopes the birch trees were in bud all ready to burst into delicate leaf. The enchantment of spring was in the air. The sun was hot. Everyone felt alert and some felt happy. The old stagers who came only for the winter were making their plans to go south. Templeton and Ivy went to see Dr Lennox together. They told him what they had in mind. He examined them; they were X-rayed and various tests were taken. Dr Lennox fixed a day when he would tell them the results and in the light of this discuss their proposal. Ashenden saw them just before they went to keep the appointment. They were anxious, but did their best to make a joke of it. Dr Lennox showed them the results of his examinations and explained to them in plain language what their condition was.

'All that's very fine and large,' said Templeton then, 'but what we want to know is whether we can get married.'

'It would be highly imprudent.'

'We know that, but does it matter?'

'And criminal if you had a child.'

3 **Quite**（=Quite right）
9 **birch trees** 樺の林　**ready to burst into delicate leaf** 柔らかい葉が萌え出る寸前　10 **enchantment** 魔法　11 **alert** はっきりしている　12 **stagers** 老練な人々　17 **in the light of this** そのことを考慮して　20 **make a joke of it** それをネタにジョークをいう
24 **All that's very fine and large** それはとてもよくわかりました
27 **imprudent** 軽率な、無分別な
29 **criminal if you had a child** もし子どもができるようなことになったら、それは罪です

'We weren't thinking of having one,' said Ivy.

'Well, then I'll tell you in very few words how the matter stands. Then you must decide for yourselves.'

Templeton gave Ivy a little smile and took her hand. The doctor went on.

'I don't think Miss Bishop will ever be strong enough to lead a normal life, but if she continues to live as she has been doing for the last eight years . . .'

'In sanatoriums?'

'Yes. There's no reason why she shouldn't live very comfortably, if not to a ripe old age, as long as any sensible person wants to live. The disease is quiescent. If she marries, if she attempts to live an ordinary life, the foci of infection may very well light up again, and what the results of that may be no one can foretell. So far as you are concerned, Templeton, I can put it even more shortly. You've seen the X-ray photos yourself. Your lungs are riddled with tubercle. If you marry you'll be dead in six months.'

'And if I don't how long can I live?'

The doctor hesitated.

'Don't be afraid. You can tell me the truth.'

'Two or three years.'

'Thank you, that's all we wanted to know.'

They went as they had come, hand in hand; Ivy was crying softly. No one knew what they said to one another; but when they came into luncheon they were radiant. They told Ashenden and Chester that they were going to be married as soon as they could get a licence. Then Ivy

2 **how the matter stands** 病状がどういうものであるか
11 **if not to a ripe old age** 長寿を全うするというほどではなくても　**sensible** 分別のある　12 **quiescent** 休止している、静止性の　14 **foci**（focusの複数形）病巣　**light up** 活性化する、活発になる　15 **foretell** 予想する　**So far as you are concerned** あなたに関しては　18 **are riddled with tubercle** 結核にかなりやられている
27 **luncheon** 昼食　**radiant** 顔が輝いている　29 **get a licence** 結婚許可を取る

turned to Chester.

'I should so much like your wife to come up for my wedding. D'you think she would?'

'You're not going to be married here?'

'Yes. Our respective relations will only disapprove, so we're not going to tell them until it's all over. We shall ask Dr Lennox to give me away.'

She looked mildly at Chester, waiting for him to speak, for he had not answered her. The other two men watched him. His voice shook a little when he spoke.

'It's very kind of you to want her. I'll write and ask her.'

When the news spread among the patients, though everyone congratulated them, most of them privately told one another that it was very injudicious; but when they learnt, as soon or later everything that happened in the sanatorium was learnt, that Dr Lennox had told Templeton that if he married he would be dead in six months, they were awed to silence. Even the dullest were moved at the thought of these two persons who loved one another so much that they were prepared to sacrifice their lives. A spirit of kindliness and good will descended on the sanatorium: people who hadn't been speaking spoke to one another again; others forgot for a brief space their own anxieties. Everyone seemed to share in the happiness of the happy pair. And it was not only the spring that filled those sick hearts with new hope, the great love that had taken possession of the man and the girl seemed to spread its effulgence on all

5 **respective** それぞれの　6 **it's all over** 結婚式が終わる
7 **give me away** 花嫁を花婿に引き渡す
8 **mildly** 優しそうに
15 **injudicious** 無分別な　19 **were awed to silence** 心を打たれて黙ってしまった　**the dullest** もっとも鈍い連中　22 **kindliness** 優しさ　**good will** 善意　24 **for a brief space** 短い時間　28 **had taken possession of** ～を手に入れた　29 **effulgence** 光輝

that came near them. Ivy was quietly blissful; the excitement became her and she looked younger and prettier. Templeton seemed to walk on air. He laughed and joked as if he hadn't a care in the world. You would have said that he looked forward to long years of uninterrupted felicity. But one day he confided in Ashenden.

'This isn't a bad place, you know,' he said. 'Ivy's promised me that when I hand in my checks she'll come back here. She knows the people and she won't be so lonely.'

'Doctors are often mistaken,' said Ashenden. 'If you live reasonably I don't see why you shouldn't go on for a long time yet.'

'I'm only asking for three months. If I can have that it'll be worth it.'

Mrs Chester came up two days before the wedding. She had not seen her husband for several months and they were shy with one another. It was easy to guess that when they were alone they felt awkward and constrained. Yet Chester did his best to shake off the depression that was now habitual and at all events at mealtimes showed himself the jolly, hearty little fellow that he must have been before he fell ill. On the eve of the wedding day they all dined together, Templeton and Ashenden both sitting up for dinner; they drank champagne and stayed up till ten joking, laughing, and enjoying themselves. The wedding took place next morning in the kirk. Ashenden was best man. Everyone in the sanatorium who could stand on his feet attended

1 **blissful** 喜びに満ちている　**the excitement became her** その興奮ぶりは彼女に似合っていた　4 **hadn't a care** 心配事などなにひとつない　5 **uninterrupted** 途切れることのない　6 **felicity** 至福、大きな幸福　**confided** 打ち明けた
8 **hand in my checks** あの世にいく
12 **reasonably** 無茶をしないように
15 **it'll be worth it** そのかいがあったというものです
19 **awkward** ぎこちない　20 **constrained** 窮屈な　**Yet** しかし　21 **at all events** ともあれ　22 **jolly** 陽気な　26 **till ten** 10時まで　28 **kirk** スコットランド教会　**best man** 新郎の付き添い役

it. The newly married couple were setting out by car immediately after lunch. Patients, doctors, and nurses assembled to see them off. Someone had tied an old shoe on the back of the car, and as Templeton and his wife came out of the door of the sanatorium rice was flung over them. A cheer was raised as they drove away, as they drove away to love and death. The crowd separated slowly. Chester and his wife went silently side by side. After they had gone a little way he shyly took her hand. Her heart seemed to miss a beat. With a sidelong glance she saw that his eyes were wet with tears.

'Forgive me, dear,' he said. 'I've been very unkind to you.'

'I knew you didn't mean it,' she faltered.

'Yes, I did. I wanted you to suffer because I was suffering. But not any more. All this about Templeton and Ivy Bishop — I don't know how to put it, it's made me see everything differently. I don't mind dying any more. I don't think death's very important, not so important as love. And I want you to live and be happy. I don't grudge you anything any more and I don't resent anything. I'm glad now it's me that must die and not you. I wish for you everything that's good in the world. I love you.'

3 **tied an old shoe on the back of the car** 車の後ろに古い靴を結びつけた（幸せな結婚生活を送れるようにというおまじない） 5 **rice was flung over them** 米がふたりに振りかけられた（ライスシャワーといって、結婚式のお祝い） 6 **cheer** 歓声
10 **miss a beat** 鼓動が飛ぶ、鼓動が止まる
14 **you didn't mean it** 本気じゃない　**faltered** つっかえながらいった
15 **Yes, I did** いや、本気だったんだ　16 **not any more** いまはちがう　17 **how to put it** どういっていいか　21 **grudge** 愚痴をいう

あとがき

　ウィリアム・サマセット・モーム（1874 - 1965）は、20世紀を代表するイギリス人作家のひとり。
　19世紀後半から20世紀前半に活躍したイギリス人作家には、ロバート・ルイス・スティーヴンソン（1850 - 1894）、オスカー・ワイルド（1854 - 1900）ジョウゼフ・コンラッド（1857 - 1924）、ラドヤード・キプリング（1865 - 1936）ハーバート・ジョージ・ウェルズ（1866 - 1946）、ジョン・ゴールズワージー（1867 - 1933）、エドワード・モーガン・フォースター（1879 - 1970）、ジェイムズ・ジョイス（1882 - 1941）、ヴァージニア・ウルフ（1882 - 1941）、デイヴィッド・ハーバート・ロレンス（1885 - 1930）、オルダス・ハクスリー（1894 - 1963）などがいる。
　それぞれに個性的で独創的な作品を書いている。
　たとえば、スティーヴンソンやキプリングは当時の国民的作家で、物語性の高い作品を美しく力強い文体で書いた。また、コンラッドは独特の（ある意味、読みづらい）文体で、海洋小説に近代的な心理描写を織りこんだ作品を発表したし、ジョイスとウルフは、当時、「意識の流れ」の作家として非常に斬新な試みを行った。ウェルズは近代科学を作品に大胆に取りこんで、フランスのジュール・ヴェルヌとともに、ＳＦ小説の父と呼ばれるようになった。
　このように、19世紀から20世紀にかけてのイギリ

スでは、多種多様な作家が活躍して、新しい方向を模索した。

そんななかでモームは、また独自の文体、手法、語り口で人々を魅了した。

モームの両親はイギリス人だったが、父親が駐仏イギリス大使館の顧問弁護士をしていたため、フランスで生まれ、10歳までそこで育った。そのためフランス語が話せたし、その後イギリスで暮らすことになるが、ドイツに留学したときにドイツ語を身につけた。また旅行が好きで、スペイン、イタリア、フランスなどを訪れ、第1次世界大戦中は志願してベルギーやスイスに行っている。また作家として執筆を続けながら、イギリスの諜報活動も行っていて、そのときの体験が、『アシェンデン』という短編集や、その他の短編に結実している。

第1次世界大戦後は、南太平洋諸島を訪れ、さらに、アメリカ、アジア、ロシアなど多くの国々を回っている。そのため、モームの作品はイギリスやヨーロッパだけでなく、世界の様々な場所が舞台になっている。

代表的な長編小説は、自伝的な小説『人間の絆』と、画家ポール・ゴーガンをモデルにした『月と六ペンス』。とくに『月と六ペンス』はベストセラーになり、その後も、世界中で読み継がれている。日本でも翻訳が何種類も出ている。

また、短編は100編を超え、時代も舞台もさまざまだし、ショートショートのような短いものから中編に近いものまで長さもさまざまだ。

あとがき

　文章は、現代人にとっては読みづらいところもあるが、当時としては平易で読みやすかったらしく、知識人や教養人だけでなく一般の人々にも広く読まれた。この本に収録した2編のうち、「征服されざる者」は比較的読みやすいが、「サナトリウム」は読みづらいと思う。

　さて、モームの作品の特徴だが、まず、なにより面白い。読み始めると、最後まで読まないと気がすまなくなる。その意味では、まさにイギリス屈指のストーリーテラーといっていい。それから、心理描写がくどくないわりに的確で、人間観察の鋭さがうかがえる。たとえば、「征服されざる者」のハンスの気持の変化などはとてもうまい。また、アネットの両親のハンスに対する態度の変化も巧みに描かれている。それは「サナトリウム」の登場人物の描き方でもまったく同じだ。

　さて、読み終えた方はもうわかっていると思うが、「征服されざる者」と「サナトリウム」は両極端といってもいいほど印象がちがう。ちがうけれど、どちらもモームだ。もしおもしろいと思ったら、ぜひ、ほかの作品にチャレンジしてみてほしい。

金原瑞人

［著者］
モーム　W. Somerset Maugham

20世紀を代表するイギリス人作家のひとり（1874-1965）。フランスのパリに生まれる。幼くして孤児となり、イギリスの叔父のもとに育つ。16歳でドイツのハイデルベルク大学に遊学、その後、ロンドンの聖トマス付属医学校で学ぶ。第1次世界大戦では、軍医、諜報部員として従軍。『人間の絆』（上下）『月と六ペンス』「雨」「赤毛」ほか多数の優れた作品をのこした。

［編者］
金原瑞人（かねはら・みずひと）

法政大学教授、翻訳家。ヤングアダルト小説をはじめ海外文学の紹介、翻訳で著名。著書『翻訳のさじかげん』（ポプラ社）ほか。訳書『豚の死なない日』（ロバート・ニュートン・ペック、白水社）『青空のむこう』（アレックス・シアラー、求龍堂）『国のない男』（カート・ヴォネガット、NHK出版）ほか多数。編著『金原瑞人 MY FAVORITES』シリーズ（青灯社）。

金原瑞人 MY FAVORITES
征服されざる者 THE UNCONQUERED /
サナトリウム SANATORIUM

2013 年 6 月 30 日　第 1 刷発行

著者　　モーム
編者　　金原瑞人
発行者　辻一三
発行所　株式会社青灯社
東京都新宿区新宿 1 - 4 -13
郵便番号 160-0022
電話 03-5368-6923（編集）
　　　03-5368-6550（販売）
URL http://www.seitosha-p.co.jp
振替　00120-8-260856

印刷・製本　株式会社シナノ
© Mizuhito Kanehara 2013
Printed in Japan
ISBN978-4-86228-065-7 C0082

小社ロゴは、田中恭吉「ろうそく」（和歌山県立
近代美術館所蔵）をもとに、菊地信義氏が作成

● 青灯社の英語の本

英単語イメージハンドブック
定価 1800円 + 税

大西泰斗（東洋学園大学教授）

1冊で基本的な英単語のイメージがすべて分かる集大成。

英語世界の表現スタイル ～「捉え方」の視点から
吉村公宏（奈良教育大学教授）　定価 1500円 + 税

英語圏では言いたいことから一直線に表現する方法を好む。日本人はうず潮型の表現を好むから海外で理解されにくい。

語源で覚える英単語 3600
定価 1700円 + 税

藤井俊勝（東北福祉大学教授）

接頭辞19種と語根200種の組み合わせで覚える、効率的な単語増強法。

金原瑞人 MY FAVORITES

金原瑞人氏の詳しい注つきで辞書なしに読む英語シリーズ。

THE BOX
定価 1200円 + 税

ブルース・コウヴィル著

英語圏で大人気の児童文学作家のやさしい短編。

変身 THE METAMORPHOSIS
定価 1200円 + 税

フランツ・カフカ著

異邦人 THE STRANGER
定価 1200円 + 税

アルベール・カミュ著